Foundations of Government and Public Administration

Volume 1

Series Editors

Jos C. N. Raadschelders, Ohio State University, Columbus, USA
R. A. W. Rhodes, University of Southampton, Southampton, UK

This series explores the values and ideals that ground a society at large and the nature of the various relations between society and government. Organised around three overarching themes – Great Thinkers about Government's Role and Position in Society, Foundations of Public Administration: Approaches to Studying Government, and Foundations of Government: Core Concepts and Ideas – the series will analyse government at its constitutional and foundational level. Such an approach is not yet mainstream, with public administration scholars more commonly focusing on the specific challenges, methods, skills, policies, and organizational structures of government's operations. This series will address that trend by providing a conceptual map of these fundamentals and making new knowledge and approaches relevant for understanding government accessible to readers by helping them to grasp their origins, meaning and relevance.

To Anna, for your constant support, unwavering encouragement, and kind patience with my never-ending writing

To Tommaso and Pietro, for bringing the freshness of the viewpoint of the new generation onto my writing with a well-mannered smile that says more than a thousand words

To Rita and Ezio, for always trusting me

Acknowledgements

All books are always collaborative endeavours, even when they take the form of single-authored monographs, and this book is no exception: I owe many people and institutions an important debt of gratitude—more than can be mentioned here, but some I wish to mention.

My first debt of gratitude goes to my home institution, the Open University UK, for generously supporting the publication in open access format of this book, as well as for supporting this endeavour in other and all incalculably precious ways all over the process of preparation of this volume. To my colleagues and students—in the department of Public Leadership and Social Enterprise and across the Business School and the Faculty of Business and Law and the wider Open University—I owe a huge debt of gratitude for the intellectual suggestions and the practical support that I have received throughout. I wish to give special thanks to Francesca Calò for believing since the outset in the importance of publishing in open access a volume which aims to foster interdisciplinary connections between fields quite far apart in the current intellectual organisation of labour within academia, and to all the members of the Open University committee who believed in the value of enabling the open access publication of this book. Heartfelt thanks also go to the library staff for providing such an impressive, always so competent, professional, friendly and supportive service to the OU community, and to me personally, in our research work. 'Reaching out' to everybody is the true essence of the mission of the Open University, and to this purpose, the

Open University has never spared its resources, even during challenging times. The support to the publication in open access format of this book is another small brick in the magnificent edifice of making knowledge available in order to change people's lives that the Open University has been building over the decades since it was established in 1969.

I wish to thank Stewart Beale at Palgrave for instantly believing in this intellectual book project when I first mentioned it in conversation, and supporting it throughout the entire process to publication, always being heedful, constructive, perceptive and insightful in the suggestions provided.

The two anonymous reviewers who reviewed the book proposal provided very encouraging and constructive advice. The third reviewer who performed the 'clearance' review of the final manuscript before publication provided a treasure trove of insights and suggestions. The series editors provided constructive suggestions and advice on the text. I am very grateful to the series editors and all the reviewers: their comments—on the structure of the book, on key aspects and core foci of it, on key reference authors—have helped make this book deeper in substance as well as, hopefully, more readable (as customary, errors are all mine).

Michele Tantardini designed and successfully rolled out the teaching of philosophy in the PhD in Public Administration programme of Penn State university, USA, and later also presented this experience of teaching 'philosophy and public administration' at the NASPAA 2025 Global Conference. I wish to thank Michele and all the participants of the session in which the experience of teaching philosophy and public administration in a doctoral programme has been discussed, and all the students at Penn State for being so encouraging towards expanding this topic systematically into PhD programmes. I am very grateful to Michele also for a thorough reading of an earlier draft of this manuscript which led to highly valuable revisions of the text (as usual, remaining errors are all mine).

Yijia Jing and all the team at the Institute for Global Public Policy at Fudan University have been very helpful to the preparation of this book, notably during my visiting professorship at Fudan and through the invitation to present selective contents of this book at the Fudan-LSE lecture series (it has been an honour for me to be a speaker at such prestigious seminar series) as well as in the organisation of the seminar "Connecting Philosophy and Public Administration: Directions of Inquiry" (patterned on this book's title and held in March 2025): I wish to thank all the participants at the workshop for very insightful and constructive comments. A lecture at SIRPA (School of International Relations and Public Affairs) at Fudan University also proved insightful in connecting aspects developed in this book with profiles of mainstream social science inquiry in the field of public administration. Dinnertime conversations I had with Tongdong Bai, Yijia Jing and Li Tang were tremendously insightful and inspirational.

At exactly the same time (potency of modern means of communication) as I was at Fudan University studying the application of Confucian thinking to politics and administration, an exchange with Mark Moore on his latest (at the time this book goes to press) book in preparation on the theory and practice of public value also proved inspirational. For me hailing from a European intellectual identity standpoint, it was so stimulating to be reading at the same time a Confucian and an American normative account of political systems, public administration and public value theory and practice, while writing this book.

I wish to thank Alfred T. Ho: an invitation to deliver a contribution at a seminar at City University of Hong Kong in March 2024 was the first occasion for me to present the initial draft of the theoretical frame outlined in this book. Ruipeng Fan, Sungmoon Kim and all the participants at the event provided brilliant questions and precious insights which nourished the further development of the intellectual work leading to this book.

The intellectual exchanges and intense collaboration with all the authors of the special issue on 'Eastern and western philosophies: Rethinking the foundations of public administration', published in the journal *Public Policy and Administration*, proved inspirational for my writing—and it taught me that the contents of this book have the potential to engage scholars and reflective practitioners from all over the world, across cultures, civilisations and intellectual traditions. Thanks go to Alfred T. Ho, Yijia Jing, Zhaopeng Li, Hongxu Liu, Yifeng Ni, Ning Liu, Luis Rubalcaba, Ryan Shane, Ernesto Solano, Li Tang, Zhang Tong, and Yi Yang.

The over forty presentations at higher education and other institutions all over the world of the book titled "Philosophy and Public Administration: An Introduction" (2017, 2nd edition 2020, Elgar Publishing) provided invaluable and continual sources of inspiration for the writing of this book: I am not able to list here the so numerous institutions that kindly invited me to present the book—let alone all the participants who took the time to attend—but I wish to recognise how their queries, questions, insights all proved inspirational for this book (remaining errors, lacunae and naiveties are all mine). I also wish to mention the institutions that supported the translation into different languages of that book: the Centro de Investigación y Docencia Económica—CIDE—in Mexico City and David Arellano-Gault who oversaw the translation into Spanish; the Chinese Academy of Personnel Sciences and the Academy of Social Sciences of China for the Chinese translation; the Instituto Nacional de Administração of Portugal and Luisa Neto for the Portuguese translation; Bocconi University and Elio Borgonovi for the Italian translation.

Feng Wang and the team at Shanghai University of Finance and Economics (SUFE) were so kind as to invite me to make a presentation of the first full-fledged version of this book in March 2025, and delighted me with very insightful questions and follow up online discussions and exchanges, notably with Ge Xun. I am very grateful for the hospitality and insights.

I am very grateful to all who have made the intellectual journey of writing this book such a nice enterprise. As the English saying goes: "The proof of the pudding is in the eating", and now the book is in press my hope is that the readers will find it useful, valuable and—perhaps—even inspirational.

London, Milton Keynes, UK
September 2025

CONTENTS

Connecting Philosophy and Public Administration: Rationale, Functions and Approaches

Abstract This chapter provides two reasons why philosophy and public administration (PA) ought to be connected more closely. The first perspective considers this connection as being constitutive and inherent: like every discipline and profession, PA is in search of its foundations, which only philosophical thinking can provide. The second perspective in connecting philosophy and PA stems from a concern for and preoccupation with the contemporary problems and multiple, interconnected and unceasing crises facing the world and society, and thence government and the public sector as a key part of society and of the possible solutions to contemporary problems. The chapter outlines the four approaches examined in this book for connecting philosophy and PA: (i) philosophy for PA; (ii) mapping backwards; (iii) aligning philosophy and PA; and (iv) philosophy of PA. The chapter then identifies the functions of philosophy applied to PA: enlightening; critical; gap filling; integrative; and normative. Finally, a research programme for connecting philosophy and PA is outlined.

Keywords Philosophy · Public administration · Functions of philosophy applied to public administration · Philosophy for public administration · Aligning philosophy and public administration · Philosophy of public administration

E. Ongaro, *Connecting Philosophy and Public Administration*,
Foundations of Government and Public Administration 1,
https://doi.org/10.1007/978-3-032-01769-7_1

CONNECTING PHILOSOPHY AND PUBLIC ADMINISTRATION: TWO MAIN RATIONALES

Why a book on connecting philosophy and public administration? We argue there are two main perspectives—supported by two distinct, albeit complementary, rationales—in connecting philosophy and philosophical thinking, on the one hand, and the field of public administration, public governance and public management (hereafter PA—more on definitions of both philosophy and PA below), on the other. The first perspective considers this connection as being constitutive and inherent: like every discipline and profession, PA is in search of its foundations, and philosophy's core preoccupation lies exactly in finding the roots and foundations of what we (human beings and the societies to which we give rise) are, what we should do, what we can know.

When seen through this lens, philosophy and PA should almost by definition be connected (since all fields of inquiry and academic disciplines should connect to philosophy) and the observation that in certain historical periods (like the one we are living in) such connection becomes tenuous gets to be seen as akin to some sort of temporary aberration, as a contingent situation brought about by some spurious, exogenous factors. Such factors may include the way in which academic groupings and career paths are organised in contemporary academia, which may have led to separating and distancing these two disciplines, which are generally grouped into different clusters—the cluster of the humanities for philosophy, a more miscellaneous clustering for PA, which may be located within political science or government departments, or in business schools, or in law schools. Other factors can reside in the pressures put by decision-makers in public sector organisations on the academia to find 'solutions that work', which are often considered as 'technical' in nature and hence afar from the core preoccupations of philosophy, hence driving the focus of the PA scholarly investigation away from philosophical interests. From this first perspective, the rationale for connecting philosophy and PA lies in remedying a contingent, temporary disconnect and reinstate a 'natural state of affairs' by providing a connection that should have always been there in the first place—connecting philosophy and PA can in this perspective be seen as 'operation back to normalcy'.

The second perspective in connecting philosophy and PA stems from a concern for and preoccupation with the contemporary problems and multiple, interconnected and unceasing crises facing the world and society, and thence government and the public sector as a key part of society. In this perspective, PA as a field of study is seen as a discipline (in itself at times deemed to undergo an 'identity crisis', Ostrom, 2008; Rutgers, 1998) which operates in a world in crisis—in multiple, interconnected crises. Climate change, the information revolution and its disruptive consequences, the return of large scale war, the risk of pandemics, the long-term legacy of the 2008 financial crisis—amongst other processes—and the multiple ways in which such processes interact, give rise to a world in poly-crisis (Tooze, 2018); and the multiple crises may deteriorate due to bad political and policy responses that are too often given, bad responses which in turn may further exacerbate such crises and trigger vicious circles difficult to break (for example, amplified economic inequalities and reduced social cohesion can trigger consensus for populist forces, which then enter government and whose governing action in turn further amplifies inequalities and deplete social cohesion, thereby nourishing the consensus for populist forces and hence reinforcing their position in government, and so forth).

In this picture, government and the public sector can be part of the solution (thence countering by means of example the narratives of those who claim they are part of the problem), but in order to attain the goal of being part of the solution, governmental, policy and administrative action require to be guided by clarity on the assumptions that inform PA theory and practice; by a critical assessment of such assumptions which may lead to revise and improve them; by novel ideas, constructs and approaches that may fill gaps in the assumptions held; by the capacity to combine and integrate various forms of disciplinary knowledge into a broader understanding of the problems to be addressed; by evaluative and normative criteria which can provide justification for public action and provide the foundations for its legitimacy. That is, in order to be part of the solution to the problems of the poly-crisis the world is facing and be able to operate to transform such crises into opportunities, PA requires philosophy and philosophical thinking, in order to: shed light on its assumptions; critically assess its assumptions and, where required, revise them; provide novel ideas, concepts and constructs to fill gaps in such assumptions; integrate diverse and at times disconnected forms of knowledge into the broader PA theory and practice; and ground and justify prescriptive and normative arguments about how governmental and administrative action should unfold, and how the public sector ought to be organised. In this second perspective, connecting philosophy and PA is a way to strengthen PA and enable it to be part of the solution to the problems of the contemporary world: it is a way of finding contemporary solutions to tackle contemporary problems and hence to transform crises into opportunities.

This book has the ambition to provide a framework for connecting philosophy (including eastern philosophy alongside western philosophy) and the field of PA in the pursuit of both rationales: the perennial one, as well as the contemporary one. A preceding book is much in the line of the first rationale: that book is explicitly a call to rediscover this perennial connection (Ongaro, 2020—the book is titled 'Philosophy and Public Administration: An Introduction', published by Elgar Publishing, and it is available open access; it has also been translated into Chinese, Italian, Portuguese and Spanish, thereby witnessing a quite widespread interest and attention for an introductory work about the contribution philosophy can provide to the field of PA). The present book aims to provide a framework of analysis of the connections between philosophy and PA that can enable to pursue both rationales: the rediscovery of the perennial linkages between philosophy and PA, while also enabling to employ and deploy philosophy to tackle specifically the contemporary challenges.

The intellectual division of labour with my previous book is that Ongaro (2020) provides an introduction to the very rationale for connecting PA to areas of philosophy (ontology, political philosophy, epistemology); the 2020 book also provides a succinct overview of key streams of philosophy in relation to its application for PA (as scholarly books in philosophy may be written in ways that are not amenable to direct application to PA problems and themes) as well as an introduction to selected philosophers and philosophies whose thought may prove to be of special significance for certain topics in the field of PA; finally, the 2020 book discusses issues of researching and teaching philosophy in PA programmes (also examined in Ongaro, 2019 and 2022). In short: that book is about rediscovering the perennial and inherent, underlying reasons for connecting philosophy and PA; this present book shifts emphasis and focus. In terms of emphasis, this book is about applying philosophy to contemporary PA problems in order to stimulate the exploration of new ideas and perspectives in developing contemporary PA. Along the way, it also has the ambition to contribute its bit, however infinitely small, not just in fostering the field of PA but also in revitalising philosophy itself, because philosophy gets fresh nourishment when its ideas and notions get applied to contemporary societal challenges and problems; in fact, as aptly noticed by the philosopher Luciano Floridi (2019, in 'Afterword—Rebooting Philosophy'), philosophy is always at risk of 'scholasticism', meaning philosophy talking about itself to itself in its own jargon, hence becoming unfruitful, incapable of bearing fruits for addressing contemporary problems; instead, the application of philosophy to contemporary problems—an important part of the solution to such contemporary problems requiring conceiving of PA to be part of the solution—can revitalise philosophy itself (indeed, philosophy has never meant to self-confine in the Ivory Tower: this rather is a drift of philosophy, and engagement with contemporary problems and issues can be immensely healthy for philosophy itself to counter any such drift). Finally as regards the differences in emphasis between the previous and the present book, the previous book provides a review of the philosophy literature (although inevitably just a drop in the ocean given the immensity of the field of philosophy)—at least western philosophy—and correspondingly the reader finds in that book classical references, mostly to the masterpieces of (excuse the pun) the masters of western philosophy; in this book, the reader will find chiefly contemporary literature and references, mostly twenty-first-century publications.

One commonality between this and the previous book is that the reader does not need to have been previously trained in philosophy to follow and appreciate the flow of the argument: we hope and think both the present book and the previous one are accessible to everyone, while keeping the highest standards of rigour in the argumentation being developed. Both books can guide the interested reader in engaging with philosophising about PA and appreciating the philosophical underpinnings of PA with increased awareness and knowledge. The reader who wants to turn such enhanced knowledge and sensitivity towards the topic of philosophy and PA into teaching applications may consider in particular the following works: an article entirely devoted to the teaching of philosophy in PA university programmes and published in one of the top journals for the teaching of PA (Ongaro, 2019); a chapter connecting researching and teaching of philosophy and PA (Ongaro, 2020, chapter 9) and a chapter on philosophy in PA published in a book entirely devoted to teaching public administration (Ongaro, 2022 in Bottom et al.). Further considerations on the significance of incorporating philosophy into PA teaching are discussed in a few paragraphs.

The other major difference between that previous book and this one is its very focus: while the 2020 book is mainly about philosophy *for* PA, while hinting also to other possible directions of inquiry, this book works out in full a framework for connecting philosophy and PA along four main directions of inquiry:

- Philosophy *for* PA: this direction of inquiry in connecting philosophy and PA is based on mobilising philosophical thinking (one or more specific philosophies or philosophical notions) to enable revisiting key PA themes (this direction of inquiry is illustrated in detail in Chapter 2).
- *Mapping backwards*, from existing PA scholarly publications to their philosophical, often implicit, underpinnings: this direction of inquiry is centred on uncovering the underlying philosophical bases of the extant PA research (Chapter 3)
- *Aligning* Philosophy and PA: this direction of inquiry is centred on the ideational bases of PA doctrines, intended as elements of knowledge, both analytical and normative, pertaining to the configuration of the administrative system, and aims at exploring the philosophical underpinnings of doctrines of reform of the public sector, such as the New Public Management, the New Public Governance and Collaborative Governance; the Neo-Weberian State; and others (Chapter 4 is devoted to this topic).
- Philosophy *of* PA: this direction of inquiry is centred on working out a philosophy of PA, which can be seen in two ways: (i) as a 'section' of a broader philosophical system; (ii) as a dedicated branch of philosophy aimed at tackling the problems and issues in PA that are philosophical in nature, and cannot be (at least not entirely) addressed through social sciences methods of inquiry; the latter direction of inquiry is delineated in this book (Chapter 5, which also concludes the book).

This book outlines the profile of each of these four directions of inquiry by also benefiting of a growing literature on the topic. This present book contributes to the growing literature on the topic by proposing and developing a framework of analysis based on four main ways—which are called 'directions of inquiry'—in which it is possible to conceptualise the interconnections between philosophical thinking and PA. The framework that is being wrought out in this book is, to my knowledge, unique in providing a comprehensive approach to analysing and making sense of the interconnections between philosophy and PA.

This book also outlines the 'functions' that philosophy applied to PA can perform, and it indicates how such functions can be performed along each of the four directions of inquiry (the functions of philosophy applied to PA are introduced at the outset of the next section, and further discussed in Chapter 2). In short, this book provides an analytical framework to map the approaches to connect philosophical inquiry and PA theory and practice, and it outlines and illustrates the functions that philosophy can perform when applied to PA. We deem that providing a broad and (in our view) comprehensive framework for connecting philosophy and PA, based on four dimensions of analysis, and outlining the functions that philosophy applied to PA can perform, along each of the four directions of inquiry, is the distinctive 'added value' of the present book.

For whom is this book written? The direct answer is that it can be relevant to a wide range of readers, scholars as well as reflective practitioners, who recognise the significance of philosophical issues and questions for their everyday concerns (be it researching and studying public administration, or the practice of it and the making of decisions in public settings). Indeed, this book makes the case and tries to provide a tool for philosophy to become part and parcel of higher education programmes in PA, undergraduate as well as postgraduate programmes (be them MPAs—Master of Public Administration or MPPs—Master of Public Policy—programmes, or specialisation tracks within an MBA—Master of Business Administration—or other postgraduate programmes—and of course in postgraduate research and PhD programmes). The argument here (using a very direct language to strengthen our case) is that we would 'betray' our students if we convey them the message that PA is a 'technical' and 'practical' field, at least without qualifying the meaning of 'technical' as well as 'practical': it is *not* technical (or to be precise 'not only' technical), as it combines techniques (which need to continue to be taught in PA programmes) with issues of values-laden decision-making problems and processes which can be appreciated only by taking also a philosophical standpoint; and it is not technical (not only) as it concerns human behaviour and decision-making whose roots are in human nature and freedom as well as culture and society, all dimensions which can be appreciated only by taking also a philosophical standpoint. And *exactly because* it is practical, PA does require of its teachers to make it explicit issues of values (normative in nature), thence of public ethics and morality and axiology, and the under-pinning political-philosophical premises of whatever is communicated to represent a pattern of 'good public administration', a notion which can only be underpinned by ideas of what it means 'living well together', hence on a conception of what is 'good' (and what is not) in life together as human beings—and the broader ontological alongside the epistemo-logical (and linguistic) premises on which it relies. PA programmes which do not even mention the philosophical underpinnings of PA are at risk of conveying the wrong message that PA can skip engaging with philosoph-ical issues; and students do intuitively realise this message to be wrong, and when they become public decision-makers they discover it for them-selves painfully, because they miss having engaged with these issues in the 'protected environment' of a classroom, and would love to 'catch up' on these issues: which is why philosophy should become part and parcel of executive education programmes in PA too. The lack of engagement with philosophy in PA programmes is a gap in the extant teaching offer which could and should be filled.

This is getting recognised more and more: as an important example, we notice that the latest (at the time this book goes to press) Subject Benchmark Statement of the Quality Assurance Agency for higher educa-tion of the UK explicitly mentions 'Philosophy of PA' as one of the listed content subfields to be included in public policy and administra-tion higher education programmes. And philosophy needs to become part and parcel also of PhD Programmes in PA and related fields: the teaching of PA in doctoral programmes has for example been experimented and rolled out at Penn State University (USA) at the time this book is being published, with an important uptake by doctoral students.

After having introduced in these initial pages the rationales for connecting PA and philosophy, we are now ready to address the key question of 'what can philosophy be used for?' and thence delineate the functions that philosophy applied to PA can perform.

THE FUNCTIONS OF PHILOSOPHY APPLIED TO THE FIELD OF PUBLIC ADMINISTRATION

Philosophy can be considered to perform certain key *functions* when applied to PA—one or more in a combined way depending on the PA problem or issues being considered. Such functions can be identified as follows (they are introduced here and further elaborated in Chapter 2):

an *enlightening* function, whereby philosophy sheds light on the guiding assumptions of PA; a *critical* function, whereby philosophy enables to revisit the guiding assumptions of PA, including by identifying possible gaps or outright contradictions in the assumptions that are held, at a given time, in the field of PA; a *gap filling* function, as philosophical knowledge can provide constructs, concepts and frameworks to fill, at least partly, gaps in PA assumptions, notions and theories; an *integrative* function, whereby philosophy sheds light on the underlying assumptions and the so-called 'philosophical residue' that is present in any social (or other) science as applied to PA, thereby enabling or at least facilitating the integration of the multiple disciplinary perspectives that are employed to address PA problems and topics; and a *normative* function, since philosophy can provide the rationale for normative-prescriptive arguments about how the public sector ought to be organised or reorganised—the 'reforms' of the public sector.

This book provides a framework to consider and appreciate the functions that philosophy can perform when applied to PA, thereby also providing a conceptual map to apply philosophy to PA. Thus, in Chapter 2 are presented and discussed in more detail the functions of philosophy applied to PA briefly previewed here; it is shown how the thought of key philosophers and philosophical streams can be applied to address PA problems and issues, thereby illustrating how philosophy can perform one or more of the functions outlined. The discussion of the findings of a number of published articles in PA that employ and deploy a philosophical perspective as a core part of their argument is used in an illustrative way to highlight the actual performance of these functions in published scholarly works. For example, we notice the integrative as well as the gap filling function that the philosophy of critical realism can perform by enabling to conjoin four distinct conceptions of what 'public value' is about into one integrated framework; or the normative function performed by philosophy when an ancient idea (both in the East and in the West) about the random selection from the population of representatives for inclusion in public decision-making processes gets applied to the public administration problem of the selection and promotion of public servants, by means of creating 'deliberative mini-publics' that can perform a role in such processes and—the argument goes—enable to overcome some of the limitations of extant public management practices. Finally, the chapter expands on the possibility of combining a range of philosophies (not just one at a time) to be able to address PA problems, as well as to, more ambitiously, match fields of philosophy with thematic areas of PA as ways of more closely interconnecting philosophy and PA.

The normative function of philosophy is especially relevant when considering the theme of what are 'good' reforms of the public sector and what it means that public services are 'better' managed after a reform of the configuration of the administrative system or the management of public services. The topic is addressed in *Chapter* 4 through the lens of the notion of 'administrative doctrines', defined as elements of knowledge with a prescriptive/normative thrust about how public administration ought to be organised. Specifically, the administrative doctrines of certain 'movements of reform' of the public sector like the New Public Management, New Public Governance, the Neo-Weberian State and the Guardian State are discussed in Chapter 4 by means of the systematic consideration of the ideational bases of such doctrines of reform, noticing that such ideational bases encompass ontological, epistemological, linguistic, ethical and political-philosophical perspectives. The chapter introduces the notion of 'ideational public governance configuration' to indicate the overall configuration of administrative doctrines and the ontological, epistemological, linguistic, ethical-moral and political-philosophical ideas which enable to conceptualise, understand, interpret and explain administrative doctrines. The notion of ideational public governance configuration is a conceptual tool to mobilise philosophical thinking for unpacking and elucidating the ideational bases of our understanding of public administration. The framework of analysis proposed in Chapter 4 may provide a further expansion and direction of development of an important, wide-ranging and expansive stream of works on public ethics (De Graaf et al., 2016; Heath, 2020; Huberts, 2014; Jorgensen & Rutgers, 2015), an area of inquiry which has been amply investigated in the PA literature—indeed perhaps it represents the only area of inquiry in the field of PA which has developed in close connection with philosophical thinking.

Prior to that, Chapter 3 discusses how to identify the philosophical premises of the extant PA scholarly works and literature, and it presents three approaches to detect and trace back the philosophical premises and underpinnings of such works: (i) by having the very authors of the public administration research to make it explicit the philosophical underpinnings of their work; (ii) by having an ex post interpretation performed by a scholar who reviews extant PA scholarly works with the aim to detect and unveil the underlying philosophical stances and premises of such works; and (iii) by investigating via bibliometric analyses the extant publications in the field of public administration and how they are influenced by academic publications in the field of philosophy. We detect in the development of this direction of inquiry the performance of the critical as well as the enlightening function of philosophy applied to PA, also paving the way for the use of philosophy to identify gaps in the extant literature (gap filling function of philosophy) as well as potentially for performing the integrative function of philosophy applied to PA.

Finally, a (yet-to-be wrought out) philosophy of PA for the twenty-first century would mediate, enable and support the performance of all five the functions of philosophy applied to PA that we have identified. *Chapter*5 outlines the contours and the features that a philosophy of PA for the twenty-first century could and should (in our view) display.

Definitions of Philosophy and Public Administration Used in This Book

The very word 'philosophy' is a product of the genius of the ancient Greeks who established and grew to vertiginous heights the 'science of reason', giving rise to philosophy as the rational investigation of reality as such, the deployment of reason and the rational faculties of humanity for attaining the fullest possible comprehension of reality as such. The very Greek language word λόγοσ (read: 'logos') indicates both 'reason' and 'word', hence it is a pivotal term in Greek philosophy to denote the capacity to apprehend reality in and through language. To dwell a moment more on the language of the people who invented philosophy, the ancient Greek word from which the English term of philosophy derives is φιλοσοφία (read 'philosophía'), which can be translated as 'love for' or 'friendship to' knowledge understood as 'wisdom', thereby indicating the speculative and contemplative character of this so noble human venture as well as the personal involvement and engagement ('love for', 'friendship') and search for the betterment of human life (by seeking to attain 'wisdom') of those human beings who pursue philosophy (we will revisit, in a few paragraphs, the contemplative thrust of philosophy as a key feature of this enterprise which originated in the West when considering similarities and dissimilarities with the thrust which underpins perspectives to philosophy that can be found in the East).

As aptly noted by Kenny (2010), philosophy is about the big questions that humanity faces (it has always faced, and it will always face), and philosophy can be characterised (and distinguished from any other 'science') by its very distinctive trait of not having a subject matter (while all sciences have a subject matter and are defined by it: physics studies the laws of movement, biology studies the living organisms, economics studies the problem of the use of scarce resources for addressing needs which can be prioritised, and so forth). What philosophy rather does have are key questions and themes, very aptly summed up by Kenny (2010) around the following ones:

- The question of Metaphysics, or Ontology, and God: 'What there is'
- The question of Soul and Mind (and Body), or Philosophical Anthropology: 'Who I am/ Who we are'
- The question of Ethics and Morality: 'How to live (well)'
- The question of Political Philosophy: 'How to live well together' ('together' meaning both within a political community—public governance—and amongst political communities across the world—global public governance)
- The question of Epistemology and Logic: 'How to know/What we know' (what is knowable, what we can and cannot know, and how we know).

While most professional philosophers will deal with specific sub-questions in their daily practice of the profession, these are key overarching questions that substantiate what philosophy is ultimately about. There are of course other questions which are also eminently philosophical, giving rise to yet other areas of philosophy (e.g. 'What is beauty?': the field of philosophy of beauty or Aesthetics, with its deep interconnections with all the other fields of philosophy): the five questions above provide a necessarily very succinct yet effective summary of key questions in philosophising, which translate into corresponding main fields of philosophy. There are also other related questions, or subtly different ways of formulating the above questions, with huge implications: e.g. the German philosopher Martin Heidegger, connecting to a long thread of philosophising, emphasised the formulation of the ontological question as: Why (is there) being rather than nothingness? And relatedly, why do I exist? Such questions complement—and are often part of the attempts to answer—the key questions delineated. It may also be noticed that Ethics/Morality and

Political Philosophy can also be referred to as 'Practical Philosophy' (a camp to which also Philosophy of Law can be ascribed, which is central to understanding the assumptions of law and legal studies in general and notably, for the field of interest in this book, administrative law), while the other branches of philosophy can be placed under the label of 'Theoretical Philosophy': while the core of our argument is that the entirety of philosophy can (and should) be applied to PA, Practical Philosophy may be the most directly applicable to the field of PA. Finally (in terms of classification of branches of philosophy), a more recent branch called 'social ontology', which can be distinguished from both 'pure' ontology and political philosophy (albeit deeply entwined with both), can find applications to PA (see Chapter 4 in this book for an application to the study of administrative reforms and their underpinning ideational bases, and Ongaro, 2020, Chapter 4 for an introduction to this branch of philosophy in view of its application to PA problems).

Importantly, all the 'modern' sciences, the individual disciplines that populate the academia have originated from philosophy and the act of philosophising and have only at a later stage detached from it, gained autonomy in terms of object of investigation and methods deployed to generate knowledge, and ultimately 'set up home' as a specific and distinct (from philosophy) discipline, all the while retaining their ultimate connection with the specific subfield of philosophy from which they derive (for example, economics derives from moral philosophy). This irreducible philosophical element present in every discipline is referred to as the 'philosophical residue'. The philosophical residue is present in any science, hence the social and other sciences that are applied to investigate PA problems and themes. The philosophical residue can be defined as the philosophical element that remains in any given field of scientific study as the irreducible questions that cannot be addressed within the confines of the specific discipline itself, with its defined object of inquiry and methods for the generation of knowledge; such questions cannot be entirely reduced to and being addressed by scientific categories of analysis. Since PA is an interdisciplinary applied field (it utilises multiple social sciences, often in combination), it requires to detect the philosophical residue not just of one but of all its constituent disciplines, as well as to understand how such philosophical issues inherent in the social sciences that are applied in the field of PA interact and combine with each other. By way of example, we may consider the critical investigation of the assumptions about the human motives (which are philosophical in nature, hence part of the philosophical residue) that are purported to drive human beings as social agents when analysed along the lines of economic science applied to PA (like in the theorisation of the bureau-shaping model, see Dunleavy, 1991), on the one hand, and when considered from the perspective of law (public law, administrative law), on the other hand, as applied to PA problems and themes; economics-based models in PA may see human beings as driven by the pursuit of self-interest and utility maximisation, while law-based models in PA may evoke sense of duty and moral compass (or absence thereof); the findings of the two disciplines may differ because of the different assumptions and perspectives they employ. Such assumptions may be similar or dissimilar, may be made explicit or be hidden and go unnoticed: philosophical inquiry enables to detect and critically examine and possibly integrate the assumptions taken by different disciplines when they are applied to PA problems and themes, hence the findings of such disciplines to the given PA problem/topic can be applied in a combined way (integrative function of philosophy) for a more holistic understanding of the problem under investigation.

It can be argued that the further away a discipline is from defining its problems in an unproblematic way and standardising its concepts in an uncontroversial way—that is, the further it is from fully setting up home as a 'normal science'—and the closer it remains to philosophy as such. In this sense, given it is widely and almost unanimously claimed that such is the case for PA, that is, that it is very far from having its problems and concepts unproblematically and uncontroversially standardised (e.g. Raad-schelders, 2005), then it can be claimed that the ties with philosophy are stronger in the case of PA than most other academic disciplines, and that the unresolved 'philosophical residue' gains even further prominence in the case of PA (Ongaro, 2020). Indeed, the inherent interdisciplinarity of PA (see below on the definition of PA) further distances it from monodisciplinary sciences (like physics or economics), since PA inherently compounds the philosophical residues of all its many constituent disciplines (that is, of all the disciplines that it applies to its subject matter: which is the functioning of government, the administrative system and public services), thereby being 'by nature' (so to speak) closer to philosophy than most other sciences. As a further consideration, it may be noticed that it is not just disciplines but more specific theories that may vary in the degree to which they have a philosophical residue, and for this reason, some PA theories are more amenable to 'philosophical treatment' than others: they contain a deeper philosophical residue; a clear example is the theory of public value, which may be seen as more inherently philosophical than other theories employed in the field of PA.

Over the centuries, philosophy has worked out a range of concepts and notions, including that of substance (the essence of a thing or entity) and accidents (ways of being of a thing that depend on another being and are not related to the nature of the thing in itself), of entity and their relations (inter-entity relations and relations of whole and part), of causality (what determines something—indicated as the 'effect'—to happen), of human freedom and individual agency (the autonomous self and the nature of human liberty), and so forth—as well as having critically reviewed and revisited 'commonsensical' notions like those of time and space, or those of mind and body—noticing that of course all notions are only apparently 'commonsensical' when seen from a philosophical standpoint. (The reader interested in a primer of philosophical concepts specifically for application to PA may wish to look at the already mentioned introductory book that precedes this one, on philosophy and public administration, Ongaro, 2020.)

In an illustrative way and concerning a notion on which we return in a few paras for its implications in relation to comparing the contribution that can come from the application to PA of both eastern and western philosophies, we briefly pick and discuss the notion of causality. The ancient Greek Philosopher Aristotle identifies four types of causes: material, formal, efficient and final. The material cause refers to the material element of which a thing is made (for example, the marble of which a statue is made—the marble being a cause of the statue, since without it the statue could not come into being), and more subtly the material cause refers to potentiality, the potential of becoming something: in fact, Aristotle goes beyond the 'simple' notion of matter as 'that which has an extension, that which occupies a volume' (this is the definition of matter used by the philosopher René Descartes), rather referring to matter as potentiality, that which has the potential of becoming something. The formal cause refers to the essence or substance of a thing, what makes it be what it is: a statue is a statue—let us define it as 'a three-dimensional artwork'—irrespective of whether it is made of marble or bronze or wood or any other suitable material; the formal cause is the form, the 'what it is' of something. The efficient cause is what makes something happen, the 'force' which effects a certain change—in the case of the statue, the sculptor operating on the material with its tools (hammer and chisel).

The final cause is the goal or end or rationale: the reason why something is brought about—in the example of the statue, the final cause can be the pursuit of beauty and/or the celebration of a ruler and/or the satisfaction of the buyer of the artwork. It goes without saying, the notion of causality has been dissected by philosophers throughout the centuries that followed Aristotle and it has been refined and extended in manifold directions, including for use in the social sciences; however, it can arguably be stated that the notion of the four causes as wrought out by Aristotle remains a key entry point to the notion of causality in philosophy.

So far so good as concerns the delineation of 'western' philosophy—in the example, the philosophical treatment of the notion of causality—for application to PA problems. Let me make an appeal to the patience of the reader to put this notion aside for a moment (we come back to it in a few paras) to now turn our attention to a challenge that comes from the East. With an oversimplification (adopted here only as starting point to introduce the issue), we can claim that eastern philosophies are different from western philosophies in a number of respects. To start with—and very important—eastern philosophies are more intimately interconnected with religion, religiosity and mysticism than is the case of philosophy in the West, where philosophy has established itself as an autonomous field of investigation driven by the use of reason and rational thinking, a domain of inquiry fully distinct from both theology and religious studies as well as from spirituality and mysticism (conceived of as the direct experience of the divine, of the connection of the human to the totality of reality attained in experiential terms). In the East, conversely, philosophy has arisen closely entwined with religion and mysticism. It can be claimed that philosophy in the East (to the extent the very term of philosophy can be utilised in this tradition of thinking) is more about giving verbal expression and form to the direct experience of the interconnectedness of the individual with reality, than about enabling the autonomous apprehension of reality by means of the force of pure reason in and by itself (again alerting the reader we deploy here an oversimplification in order to capture the key point of differentiation between eastern and western philosophy—while recognising the immense variety of conceptions of philosophy and the huge differences that can be found across what we have here lumped together as 'the East' and 'the West'). Such 'verbal expression' of the experience of interconnectedness may be wrapped in mythological language, like in the Upanishads in Hinduism (this itself being a western term coined in the nineteenth century by Sir

Monier Monier-Williams, expert of Sanskrit at the University of Oxford: an indigenous term to indicate Hinduism is *Sanatana Dharma*, which can roughly be translated as 'the eternal law'), or it can be manifested in the form of teachings for meditation—*sutras* and *mantras*. Indeed in eastern religions, and perhaps most notably in Buddhism, it is meditation which is key for the individual to attain salvation (more precisely: liberation from the cycle of re-birth or *samsara*), rather than philosophical inquiry, which may even be deemed to be an impediment on the way to liberation, as philosophical inquiry entangles the mind in quizzes and doubts which forbid to 'let go' and distract from the pursuit of mindfulness and the attainment of deep meditation (see, e.g., the interpretation of Zen Buddhism, a strand of Mahayana Buddhism which originated in China and spread to Korea and Japan and in the latter it is known as Zen Buddhism, as 'anti-philosophy', where philosophy is here intended as 'western' philosophy, see Nagatomo, 2025).

This conception of philosophy (or at least emphasis in what philosophy is concerned with) that comes from eastern thinking brings about a challenge about the very role and function of the intellect and reason (let us remind the reader here of the definition of philosophy in the West as the 'science of reason'). If in western philosophy intellect is the 'power' of the human soul that enables to attain the apprehension of reality (intellect, volition and memory are often referred to as the three key faculties or capacities of the human soul), its function may be very different in an eastern perspective, in which the role of the intellect lies rather in 'clearing the way' for enabling the direct experience of reality, in supporting a preparatory phase of casting away prejudices and errors before connection with reality can be attained, through other paths. It has aptly been noticed that philosophy in the East can be more appropriately conceived of as 'way', rather than as a body of knowledge and understanding. For example, in the interpretation of a key trait of Japanese philosophy, Kasulis (2025) notices that philosophy in the Japanese tradition is seen as an enterprise that transforms both the knower and the known through a body-mind theory-praxis, in a conception of philosophy which can be contrasted with—if not outright opposed to—the (western) idea of philosophy as a field of scholarly inquiry, to philosophy as *Wissenschaft*, where the German term of Wissenschaft points to a domain of inquiry, an area of scholarship, research and (academic) education, especially in the sense of detached knowing, 'theoretical' knowledge (the ancient Greek word for θεωρία—read 'theoria'—evokes a contemplative and speculative thrust). A Japanese (more broadly: eastern) conception of philosophy as 'way', as process in which the knower is intimately involved (through a body-mind theory-praxis), might rather be closer to the ancient Greek etymology of philosophy as 'loving wisdom', as an engaged effort to attain wisdom, although Greek philosophy also always emphasises theorising as speculation and contemplation with an element of detachment from the object being contemplated.

Can these conceptions of philosophy—eastern and western—be reconciled? This is arduous question, and one to be asked more properly of professional philosophers. What we can state here is that in our examination of the functions that philosophy applied to PA can perform (the enlightening function, the critical function, the integrative function, the gap filling function, and the normative function, previewed in the previous section and further wrought out in Chapter 2 and throughout the rest of this book), we try our best to refer to, accommodate and incorporate all these emphases and insights—eastern and western—into what philosophy is about.

There is another challenge coming from the East, more strictly metaphysical in nature (or perhaps more precisely: 'anti-metaphysical'). It relates to the key notion of dependent origination (a core concept in Buddhism—though not shared by other eastern religions and related philosophies), the notion of the interdependence and impermanence of all things, and its implications. This notion refers to the dependence of all things—whether physical or mental—on other things, including dependence of the knowing subject on all the rest, hence from this eastern perspective the knowing subject cannot be a principal autonomous entity or process, like in western philosophy is the Cartesian 'I think' which lies at the beginning of knowing for the philosopher René Descartes, or the principle of identity as 'I = I' whereby the thinking 'I think' poses itself and by posing itself it also poses the 'non-I' as claimed by the philosopher Johann Gottlieb Fichte, and hence—in Georg Wilhelm Friedrich Hegel's interpretation—the principle of identity which starts from the 'I' is the—dialectical—foundation of the entirety of reality. Conversely, the notion of dependent origination elicits major questions about the very existence of the subject as a discreet, independently existing, autonomous agent, and hence of its social agency too (and thence, as concerns the object of investigation of this book, of the social agency of public servants and of citizens-users of public services alike). Even the use and conception of language is seen differently in an eastern perspective: rather than words possessing a capacity to refer to already existing things (enabling to interpret and give meaning to them through the relationship of the signifier—the written or pronounced word—and the signified—the thing or entity to which the word refers), as it is generally assumed in a western conception, from an eastern standpoint of reality as a field of interdependent events in continuous flux, language rather arises from engagement with the field itself, and the words, reality and the speaker express the moment together as part of the flux, and the truth of words arises from their ability to confer with, rather than refer to, reality (Kasulis, 2025, sect. 5.4). We reiterate that we are here proceeding by oversimplifications to highlight points of possible contrast between perspectives and standpoints of eastern and western philosophies, and it is important to re-state that major differentiations and qualifications should be introduced within each cluster (including by noticing that the notions of dependent origination and impermanence are especially pertinent in the perspective of Buddhism and, in certain regards and within a different framework, Taoism—but not necessarily so within the frame of other eastern philosophies like, e.g. Confucianism); the point here for the purposes of this book is that such philosophical conceptions pose formidable challenges to philosophy when seen from a western perspective.

How can these perspectives (eastern and western) be reconciled? We formulate here one premise and two lines of argumentation about how to overcome this potential incompatibility (whether apparent or real). The premise is that the challenge is at the metaphysical level, the one more directly concerning philosophical preoccupations and hence of pertinence of this book. It does not pertain, however, to the level of religiosity as such: a systematic review of the scholarly literature in both the social sciences (Ongaro & Tantardini, 2023a, 2024b) and the religious studies and theology literatures (Tantardini & Ongaro, 2025) has shown how religion as both a personality system and an ideational basis, and mediated by the nature of the religious regime, does affect PA (Ongaro & Tantardini, 2023) along at least eighteen thematic areas (Ongaro & Tantardini, 2024a) and, although the (English language) literature that has been reviewed contains a lesser number of articles about eastern religions than about Christianity or Islam, there are examples of published works which illustrate how eastern religions affect different aspects of PA: from the behaviour of public managers (Dwivedi, 1990) to the level of Public service Motivation (Yung, 2014), from infusing the values of public sector organisations (Parboteeah et al., 2009) to the influence of faith leaders on local public governance (Chapman & Lowndes, 2014), from providing legitimacy to public governance (Rots, 2016) to shaping conceptions of Public Value (Ongaro & Tantardini, 2024c).

To tackle the metaphysical challenge, we propose two lines of argumentation. The first one lies in drawing a distinction between the experience of unity with the flow of becoming and the overcoming of any duality, a state that can be attained through paths like deep state of meditation (a 'state' which, for example, in Zen Buddhism is designated as non-discriminatory wisdom, a state in which the Zen practitioner can trans-descend and which transcends the perceptual reality we experience in everyday life, and which poses challenges for western philosophical notions of being, self, time and space—amongst others), on the one hand, and the everyday life, on the other hand, where 'normal' sensorial experience and normal science continue to apply. Since every encounter of citizens with public administration and public services occurs in the everyday life, it could be argued that the metaphysical challenge of conceiving of reality as a field of interdependent events in continuous flux is indeed a challenge at the ontological level, but not something the scholar and the practitioner of PA should concern themselves about. This point is effectively illustrated in the profiling of the Zen person discussed in Nagatomo (2025, sect. 8.1) in which, in the commentary to a passage of the Zen dialogue between Zen Master Ungen and a fellow practitioner, when Ungen is making a cup of tea, the dialogue runs as follows:—Practitioner: "To whom are you going to serve the tea you are preparing?"—Ungen: "There is the person who wants it"—Practitioner: "Can't the person who wants it make the tea himself?"—Ungen: "Fortunately, I am here to do it for him". In this dialogue, 'person' designates a Zen person who has attained non-discriminatory wisdom, while 'you' designates those who remain in the everyday world. The former is a 'trans-individual' while the latter is an 'individual': the former cannot 'make the tea himself' because he or she is not incarnate like the individual who remains in the everyday world, who continues to live in the perceptual world according to everyday commonsensical patterns of behaviour (like being able to use what nowadays would be a kettle to make a tea). The Zen master avails him or herself of both of these perspectives—she or he is extraordinary in having attained wisdom, while at the same time being quite ordinary in appearance and availing her/himself of the everyday perspective when required: to make a tea or, in the case of more direct pertinence for the subject of this book, to make, co-produce or use a public service.

The second line of argumentation to tackle the metaphysical challenge undertakes another path, arduous yet potentially fruitful. An integrative path can in fact be envisaged, one which engages with philosophical concepts and perspectives both eastern and western and pursues the path of integrating such notions into broader frameworks—at least within the much more modest remit of the application of these concepts to the field of PA which is the humble preoccupation of this book, leaving aside, to the extent this is possible, addressing the broader and more fundamental underlying philosophical issues—questions that have occupied the brightest minds for millennia.

How can, then, be reconciled the perspective typically adopted by philosophies and philosophers where Buddhism has historically been more influential, e.g. Japanese Philosophers who view reality as field—viewing reality in terms of a complex, organic system of interdependent processes, a system that includes themselves as knowers (Kasulis, 2025, sect. 5.2)—with views of reality centred on notions like the autonomous existence of entities (their substance and attributes) and of the self-conscious soul (the thinking subject) and the explanation of change (or the absence thereof) at the physical, social, psychological and metaphysical level through notions like Aristotle's four causes (the already introduced western notion to which we can now return)? Since we are examining these arduous philosophical problems in relation specifically to the application of philosophical concepts to PA, we can afford to discuss such issues in relation to specific PA problems rather than in abstract and purely philosophical terms.

One of these PA problems concerns how to conceptualise the notion of 'context'—usually referring to the societal, cultural, political and administrative context—and the ways in which it affects continuity and change of public administrative systems and public services and their reform—a major strand of research and inquiry in the field of PA (Pollitt, 2013; Pollitt & Bouckaert, 2017). The notion of context is fraught with philosophical implications, thereby making it a topic of interest for analysis from a philosophical standpoint (Ongaro, 2026). What kind of causality applies when studying contextual influences? One useful notion is that of multiple conjunctural causation, in which 'outcomes are analyzed in terms of intersections of conditions, and it is usually assumed that any of several combinations of conditions might produce a certain outcome'

(Ragin, 1987, p. x and chapter 2). It is centred on multiple intersecting conditions linking features of context and process to certain outcomes and in which different conditions combine in different and sometimes contradictory ways to produce the same or similar outcomes. While still firmly within a western philosophy-derived notion of causation, because it distinguishes between causes and effects rather than assuming interdependence of all things with all other things, the notion of multiple conjunctural causation may possibly represent a tentative bridge with the notion of universal interconnectedness, at least for the practical and limited purpose of application to analyses of a PA problem like the question of how a notion like context can be dealt with to understand its influence on the functioning of administrative systems. In fact, the notion of context by its very transparent etymology suggests the image of a tissue (Rugge, 2013, pp. 44–45—the Latin *contextere*, from which the English word 'context' is derived, in fact means 'to weave together'), of something which is woven (interconnected) into something which is (indefinitely) broader. Indeed, the notion of context is intriguing in terms of exploring bridges between notions in western philosophy and concepts from eastern philosophies for a range of reasons. In fact, context 'denotes an object of an undetermined extension' as 'there is always a broader context' (Rugge, 2013, p. 44): contextual influences are amenable to being studied through a range of conceptualisations of causation grounded in western philosophy: the Aristotelian four causes, multiple conjunctural causation, probabilistic causation (Ongaro, 2013, pp. 198–201), primary and secondary causes—and yet the very notion of context denoting an undetermined (indefinite?) extension evokes interconnectedness and interdependence of things on other things. It may also evoke a holographic paradigm of analysis, typical of eastern thinking whereby the whole (holo-) is considered to be inscribed (-graph) in each of its parts (Kasulis, 2025, sect. 2.2), a paradigm which is not alien to western thinking (consider Neoplatonism whereby each unit, and notably each person, is considered to be a micro-cosmos and to reflect the entirety of reality within itself): analysing phenomena in context is an approach to detecting the connections between a unit (the focused object of analysis), that is, what is determined in its extension, and the undetermined extension of which it is part and that it reflects. Moreover and relatedly, the notion of 'context denotes one object, but in fact evokes two of them [t]here is no context without a "contexted", an object that is or has to be put into a context' (Rugge, 2013, p. 44), thereby suggesting a relational view of reality, evoking if not outright pointing to reality as a field.

Combining these elements of reflection, there appears to be an opening to envisage a path(way)—at least within the frame of the confined application of philosophy to a delimited set of concerns like those in and of PA—towards fruitfully combining western and eastern philosophical notions to study PA (Ongaro, 2021), towards a truly global appreciation of the application of philosophy to PA. The end result of such effort can have global reach, as it encompasses and is open to the wider range of philosophical perspectives and pursues a critical analysis to integrate them, without being globalist, that is, it does not reduce or subsume different perspectives into one viewpoint—rather it strives to attain a higher-level integration of the contribution that each perspective can provide, achieved not in a syncretistic mode but through critical inquiry in the Kantian sense, through an approach that strives to attain synthesis wherever possible while also contemplating the possibility of rejecting options which are deemed contradictory or unacceptable on logical-ontological ground. This way, a range of conceptualisations of causation grounded in western philosophy—the four causes, multiple conjunctural causation, probabilistic causation, primary and secondary causes—can be combined with paradigms grounded in eastern philosophy—interconnectedness and interdependence,[1] holographic relations—in view of a broader and more

---

[1] The notion of interconnectedness is central also in different perspectives to those associated with Buddhism and certain eastern religions and philosophical systems. In the East, it is central in Hinduism (Sanatana Dharma), albeit in Hinduism the existence of the autonomous self (soul or *atman*) is a central tenet, and all that exists has its self (atman), and all souls are interconnected and ultimately a manifestation of the absolute principle, *Brahman*. In the West, interconnectedness is central to Christianity, notably in Catholicism in the key notion of the Communion of Saints—the communion in Christ of all people and of all things who belong to God, who are all interconnected in and through Christ (the Second Person of the Holy Trinity), who is the Vine to whom all those who belong to Christ partake as its shoots, while maintaining one's own autonomous self (in full unity of soul and body, hence in full psychosomatic or body-mind unity—this happening according to the Christian faith as the end of times when the *parusía*—the return of Christ on earth / in this world—will occur and will bring about the resurrection of the body of all human beings: this is marvellously visualised in the most famous painting by Michelangelo Buonarroti in the Sistine Chapel in the Vatican); this consideration provides an important bridge with the notion of body-mind theory-praxis that we have seen in relation to eastern philosophies, and it is also a powerful reminder that the perspective of mind-body unity has been amply considered also in western philosophy, whose richness cannot be simplistically reconducted to the divarication of Cartesian ascendence of mind

encompassing potential synthesis. A path of inquiry for the application of philosophy to PA characterised by an integrative thrust is therefore envisaged in this book in which we aim to dissect the connecting points between philosophy and PA and the functions of philosophy for PA in an encompassing way (as encompassing as possible) by relying on both western and eastern thinking, with all their huge richness of thought and understanding and internal variety (in the same line of analysis is situated the collective work published in the special issue guest edited by Ho and Ongaro, 2025, titled 'Eastern and Western Philosophies: Rethinking the Foundations of Public Administration'; for an argument about the benefits of integrating eastern and western philosophical perspectives for application to PA, see specifically the editorial introduction, Ongaro & Ho, 2025).

We can now turn to the definition of PA that we use in this book. We use the acronym PA to encompass three notions: public administration, public management and public governance. We deem the framework wrought out in this book for connecting philosophy and PA to apply to all three the notions (an argument originally developed in Ongaro, 2020, chapter 1, pp. 9–18 in particular, from which we draw in this section), which are then placed collectively under the umbrella of PA (we indicate in the text whenever we are singling out one or the other, if and when a certain aspect of the connection with philosophy pertains more specifically to it). Starting from the notion of public administration, there seems to be wide consensus amongst scholars in the field that it can be defined as

and body, of the separation if not outright opposition of *res cogitans* (literally: the 'thinking thing') and *res extensa* (literally, the 'extended thing', the thing which occupies space). This conception provides room for interpreting the notion of the autonomous self, that is, of individual or personal freedom, as relational freedom, that is, a freedom that acquires its full meaning in the encounter and relation with the freedom of fellow human beings as well as the liberty of God, who in the perspective of the Christian faith (and the Abrahamic faiths more broadly) engages into a covenant with humanity in which God, in a sense, fulfils his liberty by freely choosing to bind Himself to humanity thereby living a relational form of freedom, one which chooses to constrain itself for love of the others, of all creatures.

In relation to the key topic for this book of the interconnection of faith, religion and philosophy, we notice that the Christian faith and the Greek philosophy combined in the Patristic philosophy to complement each other (a key element for conjoining faith and Greek philosophical reason is in the Gospel according to John in which Christ is referred to as the *Logos*). While philosophy established itself in the West as an autonomous field of inquiry relying on the power of reason, it also profoundly intertwines with religion and faith, in a mutual nourishment.

a subject matter, defined by its subject (Dunleavy & Hood, 1994; Ferlie et al., 2005; Ongaro & van Thiel, 2018; Perry & Christensen, 2015; Pollitt, 2016; Raadschelders, 2005) rather than being defined by its focus on one category or dimension of natural or social phenomena or by its methods (which are borrowed from other disciplines and often combined, as public administration displays an inherent openness to methodological pluralism). A subject matter is defined by the terrain it covers, all the while remaining a discipline in the sense of Wissenschaft, a field of scholarly inquiry, study, education (and in this sense being an academic discipline in its own right).

In distinguishing between public administration and the second notion that we place under the umbrella of PA, that is, the notion of public management, Pollitt and Bouckaert (2017) notice that one way of qualifying the notion of public administration is by emphasising its concern with the processes of preparation, promulgation/enactment and enforcement of the law, also in view of the consideration that a distinctive trait since Weber's theorisation lies in conceiving of public administration as operating under conditions of legal domination, whereby the law is the legitimate source of power in the 'modern' world, rather than charisma or tradition (Rosser, 2018); to differentiate from the notion of public administration, Pollitt and Bouckaert observe that the notion of 'public management' has a different emphasis: rather than on the role of law, public management is defined by its focus on the relationship between resources consumed and results produced by public organisations public administration and public management are in this respect different mappings of the same terrain (Dunleavy & Hood, 1994). Finally, the notion of public governance, which we also include under the label of PA throughout this book, is used to refer to the broader processes of steering of society by public institutions and engaging non-governmental actors into public policy, to distinguish from the stricter focus on governmental authoritative decisions and administrative processes that are captured by the label of public administration (Pierre & Peters, 2000) the notion of governance also refers to the broader formal and informal rules, conventions, practices and beliefs in place in a given political regime.

So far, we have addressed the question of defining PA from the lens of PA as a science, in the sense of field of scholarly inquiry, study and education. PA is also, on an equal footing and in an equally constitutive way, a profession (Frederickson, 1980): PA is being practised by millions of people across the public administrative systems and public services all over the world; in this perspective the aim of PA would then be optimising public administration in the widest sense, that is, making the state and all public institutions work as legitimately, fairly, effectively and efficiently as possible (Bauer, 2018).

Next, PA can be seen as an 'art' (Lynn, 2006)—and indeed the arts (the fine arts) should not be seen only as metaphor but as a proper source for understanding the nature of PA (Bouckaert, 2025; De Graaf & van Asperen, 2025; Drechsler, 2025; Ongaro, 2025).

Finally, PA has been defined as 'humanism', specifically as a form of practical humanism (Ongaro, 2020, chapter 1). Biancu and Ongaro (2025) specifically interrogate in what sense it is possible to speak of humanism of and for PA, and they revisit defining issues about the notion of humanism: as a historical and historiographic term, as a synthesising cultural category, and as an axiological term. They then reflect on how humanism intended as a mythical and axiological reference can provide a horizon of sense within which PA can be studied and practised, and they notice how the notion of humanism can operate as a synthesising and generative category at the core of a constellation of notions—like human dignity and human rights—which require being continuously renegotiated while remaining universally shared by humankind and in need of being continually upheld. They conclude that such conception substantiates a notion of public administration as practical humanism. We may further notice this conception is very much in line with Waldo's conception of the nature of the discipline of public administration (1948/ 1984), a conception which has recently been revisited by Overeem (2025) highlighting the inherently philosophical, specifically Socratic, stance of Waldo, thereby proposing a reading of Waldo's approach and stance to PA as inherently philosophical.[2]

In a published work unfolding in the form of a dialogue by the author of this book and a then high-level official of the European Commission (Dewandre & Ongaro, 2022/2024), the case for bringing PA back

---

[2] Notably drawn from political philosophy and political theory; we may further observe that we could also use the expression 'public affairs' here, noticing however that public affairs (i) is broader than the specific focus on the triad of public administration, public management and public governance which is the focus of this book, and (ii) that public affairs encompasses political philosophy too, so the notion of public affairs encompasses both the fields of knowledge that this book aims to connect: it refers to both 'PA' and 'Philosophy', while at the same time also denoting other areas of scholarly inquiry and practice that fall beyond the scope of this book.

to its humanistic roots has been made in strong terms by recalling the always valid admonitions that Hannah Arendt (1951/1958) issued to the contemporary rulers of her time when she referred to the death of Socrates as the death of wisdom in both public governance and society at large: from this consideration stems her call to rediscover philosophical wisdom alongside and in a sense over technical expertise as the only way forward for a better and more humane society and public governance. Her call resonates as part and parcel of the rationale for both this book and the one that precedes it (Ongaro, 2020), whose overarching thrust is to (re-)introduce philosophical knowledge into the study of PA in a more systematic way, and with it re-bring philosophical wisdom (the wisdom that derives from philosophical knowledge and understanding) into public governance.

Philosophy and PA: A Developing Research Agenda and Scholarly Programme

We conclude this chapter by wrapping up on the framework proposed in this book about how to connect philosophy and PA along four directions of inquiry and revisiting key issues encountered when attempting to more systematically connect Philosophy and PA. In this final section, we at first consider the issue of the responsibility (in the spirit of the Philosopher Paul Ricoeur's ethics of responsibility) of those scholars and whoever is pursuing such endeavour, to then discuss the conditions under which the endeavour of more systematically interconnecting philosophy and PA may be pursued along all four the directions of inquiry outlined throughout the volume, and delineate the contours of a research agenda which may hopefully become a shared and collegially owned scholarly programme of investigation longer-term.

To introduce the issue of responsibility in undertaking the academic enterprise of connecting philosophy and PA, I would like to recall a question that was asked when presenting at a research workshop the initial contours of what later would become this book: 'Why open the gate and flooding PA, a practical discipline with its feet on solid 'technical' ground, with the quagmires of philosophy?' The implication of the question: 'Isn't it dangerous to bring into PA the philosophical never-ending querying, with its entailed risk of entangling PA into the morass of philosophical quizzing and doubting, its inherent risk of 'scholasticism', and ultimately the danger of getting PA to be shackled and bogged down, paralysed in the quagmire of philosophical questioning and not able anymore to advance through accumulation of (empirical) knowledge and the elaboration of solid, strictly social scientific, verifiable claims?' (I am indebted to Sungmoon Kim for eliciting my reflections on this point and to Alfred T. Ho and City University of Hong Kong for hosting the workshop during which this discussion unfolded.)

The question, and the challenge it entails, is serious. Indeed, any intellectual enterprise mobilising philosophical thinking should never be done light-heartedly—quite the opposite, it is something that should be done responsibly, with the humility, restraint and awareness of one's own limitation, as well as the kindness and gentleness, displayed by the Philosopher Paul Ricoeur and his approach rooted in an ethos of responsibility. Moral judgement can be attributed to the human self, and we can be morally judged and hence held responsible for our own actions—including the intellectual action of scholarly writing and teaching—actions which should be assessed not only on the bases of the conviction with which they are undertaken and whether they are inherently 'appropriate', but also by the consequences they can engender (hence an ethics of responsibility). It would therefore be remiss to be naïve or dismissive about this 'risk area'.

In order to seriously engage with this important concern, three interconnected claims can be put forward for why bringing back the connections of PA with the field of philosophy is a worthy enterprise, also from an ethics of responsibility viewpoint—leaving it to the readers to judge the value of these claims. The first claim is grounded on a (very unphilosophical) matter-of-fact constatation: that contemporary PA has become so a-philosophical, that it has gone so far down the road of overlooking or outright ignoring and disregarding philosophical thinking altogether, that it may well be the moment of compensating for it, of offsetting at least to some extent this drift. Banal as the formulation of this argument may be, the point here is that—like in medicine—it is also a matter of dose: were contemporary PA completely absorbed by philosophical preoccupations, and the scholarly works in the field of PA entirely concerned with philosophical questioning to the detriment of the contribution that other disciplinary perspectives can bring to the field, it would probably not be responsible to issue a call for connecting further philosophy and PA. However, such is not the case: the field of PA is strongly rooted in the social sciences, and rightly so. Indeed, most of the calls in PA over the past decades and since at least the aftermaths of World War

II have been about strengthening the contribution to PA as an interdisciplinary field of one or the other social science that was considered to have been overlooked in the preceding period: so, over time, movements of opinion have emphasised the contribution of management (over the alleged previous dominance of law in the field of PA), the contribution of political science (over the alleged risks of managerialism in PA, notably at the zenith of the New Public Management), of social psychology and the experimental research methods coalescing around the label of behavioural public administration (over the limitations of all the previously emphasised disciplines), and so forth. However, none of these calls has, to our knowledge, ever involved philosophy and philosophical thinking. Put simply, calls for new disciplines have plucked from the social sciences, and more recently from the STEM (Science, Technology, engineering and Mathematics), driven by the impressive advances in computer sciences and digital technologies, but they have forgotten the humanities and the contribution they may provide to contemporary PA. Indeed, interdisciplinarity is constitutive of PA and strengthening interdisciplinarity in and for PA demands to encompass the humanities as well (a case being made in a collective work by over twenty scholars, see Ongaro et al., 2025a), and philosophy is king and pivotal in the realm of the humanities. Therefore, given the humanities at large and philosophy specifically have been overlooked over many decades now, it may be high time for issuing a call to bring back philosophy and the humanities into PA.

This constatation brings us to the second and connected claim for why contemporary PA may benefit of philosophy. The field of PA has over its history oscillated between the two poles that constitute its dual nature as both an applied field, an assemblage of solutions to practical problems, and as an academic field, a scholarly discipline within academia (Wagner & Raadschelders, 2025). As an academic field, and one which is inherently interdisciplinary in nature (as amply discussed throughout this chapter), the status and standing of PA within the academia can only be strengthened by the solidification of its connections with a discipline like philosophy, *the* academic discipline *par excellence*, at least in the West. An argument can therefore be put forward that the flourishing of PA within academia may also depend on the strength of its connections with other established disciplines, chief amongst them being philosophy. This may perhaps be seen as an instrumental argument, concerned about the flourishing of PA as an academic field based on the constatation that connecting with philosophy may be instrumental to this purpose, yet it is not irrelevant since the flourishing of PA as an academic field may generate the research and educational opportunities—attracting research funding, attracting students—which may in turn engender a virtuous cycle of development of the field which spills over to the 'real world' of public administrative systems functioning and public services being managed better. It is a goal of this book to contribute to strengthen the status of PA as an academic discipline—its standing and recognition. That said, connecting with philosophy provides PA with more than that: it enables PA to expand its boundaries.

This consideration connects to the third claim we put forward for why PA needs philosophy: this is based on the (philosophical) consideration that 'philosophy is always there', including in PA. In fact, PA—like all human enterprises—does have guiding assumptions: we may not notice them, given how deeply embedded they are in our own thinking, but they are there: our philosophical presuppositions determine and shape what we think and how we think; philosophy is already there serving PA scholars and practitioners alike. We said earlier on that PA has become a-philosophical, but this is in a sense impossible, as philosophical assumptions are always there, although they may be implicit and get unrecognised. We may just not be aware of them, and if such is the case, then this means that PA has drifted along the road of basically countenancing and assuming only a few philosophies (philosophical streams) as acceptable, ruling out the others—without any rationale for making such a self-limiting move.

The three philosophical strands that have possibly found their way into PA over the past decades are Positivism (which, as insightfully argued by Whetsell & Shields, 2011, has come to enjoy a status of 'quasi default philosophy' for many scholars in the field of PA, perhaps also driven by a thrust towards explanation and causality inspired by an emulative— of the natural sciences—approach which seems to be quite dominant in PA, as it is or has been in other social sciences or humanities, see Atkinson, 1978, for historiography; and see also Beaton et al., 2024, on the 'burden of objectivity' that this approach may place on the shoulders of scholars of PA), Pragmatism (see, inter alia, Ansell & Boin, 2019; Shields, 1996, 2008; Whetsell & Shields, 2011; Whetsell, 2025), and Relativism-Constructivism (see, amongst others, Box, 2007; Catlaw & Treisman, 2014; Farmer, 2005; Fox & Miller and notably their joint work Miller & Fox, 2007). These three perspectives applied to PA have been recently reviewed in Ongaro and Yang (2024), a work which also makes the case for introducing Critical Realism more forcefully into PA. Other perspectives surface occasionally: chiefly amongst them the Aristotelian-Thomist Realist philosophical tradition, which is closely connected to Critical Realism, and which is occasionally, albeit most often implicitly, brought up in rigorous yet also super-parsimonious ways by certain leading scholars (at least so I interpret some works of scholars like Geert Bouckaert, Wolfgang Drechsler or Guy Peters—and indeed also some of my own works, e.g. Ongaro, 2009, 2024). And this is all, or almost all, as concerns the explicit and self-conscious application of philosophy to PA. The risk is therefore that PA gets de facto dominated by a few philosophies, and it ends up missing out on the contribution that many other philosophical traditions with deep roots can bring to the field. This is a problem which demands to be addressed, in line with the stated approach of an ethos of responsibility in engaging with this venture of introducing philosophy into PA. We deem it would be remiss to not facilitate the connection between PA and a broader range of philosophical streams, as this precludes the field of PA from benefiting of their contribution; and not encompassing such other philosophies would leave the field of PA 'biased', not towards not-philosophy (which is ultimately impossible as philosophy is already there in every human activity) but rather towards a limited and ultimately narrow range of philosophical strands (however important each of them is in its own terms), which do not get critically appreciated and questioned against the contribution that other philosophies can offer and provide to PA. This is indeed the rationale for this book: providing a framework for connecting the field of philosophy and the field of PA that can facilitate the development of bridges between the widest range of philosophical streams and traditions, on the one hand, and the field of PA in its entirety, on the other. This book attempts to enable these connections to happen, as well as along the way and as most welcome 'by-product' (so to speak) to also enable to revisit critically the contribution of the few philosophies which have already somewhat found their way into PA.

This is why it is worth delineating the steps for developing a research agenda for individual scholars or reflective practitioners who may deem it worth pursuing the establishment of closer connections between philosophy and PA as part of their research work and their commitment to public service. Such research could become a scholarly programme proper, a broader collective and collegiate effort. How to develop this research agenda and scholarly programme further? There are practical and theoretical steps that can be considered.

The reader may be interested in starting from the practical ones, after having been exposed to theoretical considerations earlier on in this chapter and with many more to come throughout the rest of this book. A first practical point regards how to build networks of teams of scholars (and practitioners) engaged in this inquiry; part of the problems lies in the fact that working on such an interdisciplinary venture like the intellectual effort to strengthen connections between philosophy and PA can in some regards be likened to swimming against the tide: academic incentive structures are likely to run against the bridging of seemingly unrelated fields; across-the-board constraints on obtaining funding may play out (especially for a line of activity that does not appear at face value oriented to developing knowledge which can translate into skills for the job market, more and more a key requirement for receiving funding in contemporary academia); engaging into such efforts may also bring with it reputational issues for scholars as blending findings of these two fields may be very challenging because these academic fields are so distant in their thrust, academic status, career paths, conventions of what is 'highest standard of science', and so forth. However, realism in appraising the challenges ahead is important but should not lead to overlooking the opportunities that lie in undertaking interdisciplinary efforts at bridge-building: building connections between academic fields is deeply enriching, first and foremost for those who engage into this venture. A green field opens up for those who engage into connecting these two fields and embark in such interdisciplinary venture, who may become leaders in a new area of inquiry and develop academic standing in a distinct area, as well as a reputation as academic bridge-builders. Interdisciplinary work also seems to attract a lot of interest from students, practitioners and the public at large: PA scholars who engage with foundational issues are likely to attract much more interest from their audience than just by speaking about more conventional PA topics and themes; and philosophy scholars who, by connecting with PA, become able to also bring to the attention of the audience connections with 'actual' contemporary problems, may reach out to their audience more effectively.

Journal editors may also potentially play a big role in the process of establishing the interdisciplinary connections between philosophy and PA: for example, by demanding of prospective contributors to make their philosophical assumptions more explicit when submitting a contribution, perhaps ideally as a 'standard section' of their submission, like the methods section or the discussion section which are standard component in every PA publication. Indeed, the readership of a journal article may well wish to know what the underlying assumptions of a given piece of research are, exactly like they demand to know about the methods employed to generate knowledge or the implications of the findings of the research (findings which in their turn can be better interpreted if the underlying philosophical assumption which drove and informed the research in the first instance are made explicit and elaborated upon by the author of the article).

These are some of the practical steps to advance the programme of connecting philosophy and PA. As regards theoretical considerations, we suggest two approaches in developing this research programme. The first one is exploratory: one approach to make this research programme both very attractive (for scholars and practitioners alike) and very fruitful is by interconnecting it with the cutting-edge subfields of inquiry in PA, the ones that are 'the next big thing', and when the limits get reached about what can be studied with empirical methods or logical-mathematical reasoning (i.e. standard science) applied to PA problems, then usher in philosophy to tackle the issues that cannot be addressed with standard scientific methods and deploy the intellectual power of philosophy, thereby highlighting the functions of philosophy for PA: enlightening; critical; gap filling; integrative; and the capacity of philosophy to address issues and questions that are normative in nature. For example, at the time, this book goes to press the 'next big thing' is the impact of artificial intelligence on public administration and public governance and the dramatic changes to state-citizen interactions driven by the disruptive innovations occurring in digital and algorithmic governance. A research programme centred on connecting philosophy and PA may complement and supplement the scholarly literature by enabling to shed light on aspects of digital governance that are philosophical in nature and ethical (hence inherently normative) in thrust. In working out the contours of a philosophy of PA for the twenty-first century (Chapter 5), we systematically resort to philosophy of information, a recent and novel branch of philosophy, using it both as a pattern and also for its potential to enable connecting philosophy and PA around issues which are especially salient and relevant for the contemporary debates in PA.

The second approach, in a sense the one most directly flowing from this book, lies in using the framework wrought out in this book as an orientation map and picking and developing each of the four directions of inquiry outlined here further. Each of the next chapters provides elements hopefully useful for how this can be done in relation to the direction of inquiry presented and discussed in the chapter. So, in philosophy for PA (this direction of inquiry is developed in Chapter 2), indications are provided about how to expand the range of philosophies applied and the range of PA problems investigated. In mapping backwards from scholarly works in PA to their underlying philosophical assumptions (this direction of inquiry is delineated in Chapter 3), indications are provided on how to further expand the coverage in the recognition of the philosophical assumptions of extant PA works. In aligning doctrines for the reform of the public sector with their ideational underpinnings (the direction of inquiry analysed in Chapter 4), further clusters of doctrines may be considered, and more detailed analytical connections between administrative doctrines and their ideational bases may be developed. And, finally and crucially, a key pillar of this research programme rests in working out in full a philosophy of PA for the twenty-first century, whose features and contours are outlined in Chapter 5.

If, as the English saying goes, 'the proof of the pudding is in the eating', then it is now high time to draw to an end this introduction and overview chapter, and let the reader turn to Chapters 2–5, dedicated to outlining the four directions of inquiry in connecting philosophy and PA that substantiate the framework of analysis that this book works out, starting from philosophy for PA, to which Chapter 2 is dedicated, followed by the backwards mapping approach that is detailed in Chapter 3, the aligning of philosophy and PA—aligning doctrines for the reform of the public sector with their inherent philosophical premises and ideational bases—the direction of inquiry to which Chapter 4 is dedicated, and, in the most classical 'last but not least' (to conclude with another English adage), the delineation of the key traits of a philosophy of administration, the final direction of inquiry in connecting philosophy and PA that is proposed in this book, which is the task for the concluding Chapter 5.

REFERENCES

Ansell, C. & Arjen T. Boin. (2019). 'Taming Deep Uncertainty: The potential of pragmatist principles for improving strategic crisis management', *Administration & Society, 51*(7), 1079–1112.

Arendt, H. (1951/1958). *The Origins of Totalitarianism*. Boston, MA: Houghton Mifflin Harcourt

Atkinson, R. F. (1978). *Knowledge and Explanation in History: Introduction to the Philosophy of History*. Cornell University Press.

Bauer, M. (2018). Public Administration and Political Science. In E. Ongaro & S. van Thiel (Eds.), *The Palgrave Handbook of Public Administration and Management in Europe* (pp. 1049–1065). Palgrave Macmillan.

Beaton, E. E., Raadschelders, J. C. N., Wilson, G. D., Khurana, S., & Leach, N. R. (2024). The Yoke of Objectivity in Public Administration (and Beyond). *Perspectives in Public Management and Governance, 7*(3), 89–100.

Biancu, S., & Ongaro, E. (2025). Benevolence, Public Ethics and Public Services: Revisiting Public Value, Public Service Motivation, and Models of Public Administration Through the Ethics of Supererogation. In E. Ongaro, G. Orsina, & L. Castellani (Eds.), *The Humanities and Public Administration: An Introduction* (pp. 68–78). Edward Elgar.

Bouckaert, G. (2025). Mind the Gap: A Strategy to connect Humanities (Arts) with Social Sciences (Public Administration). In E. Ongaro, G. Orsina, & L. Castellani (Eds.), *The Humanities and Public Administration: An Introduction* (pp. 253–274). Edward Elgar.

Box, Richard C. (2007). *Democracy and Public Administration*. Armonk, NY: M.E. Sharpe.

Catlaw, T.J. and Treisman, C. (2014). Is 'Man' Still the Subject of Administration? Antihumanism, Transhumanism, and the Challenge of Entangled Governance. *Administrative Theory & Praxis, 36*(4), pp. 441–65.

Chapman, R., & Lowndes, V. (2014). Searching for Authenticity? Understanding Representation in Network Governance: The Case of Faith Engagement. *Public Administration, 92*(2), 274–290.

De Graaf, G., Huberts, L., & Smulders, R. (2016). Coping with Public Value Conflicts. *Administration and Society, 48*(9), 1101–1127.

de Graaf, G., & van Asperen, H. (2025). The Arts and Public Administration: How Artworks Can Be a Source of Knowledge, Inspiration, Motivation, and Understanding in Public Administration. In E. Ongaro, G. Orsina, & L. Castellani (Eds.), *The Humanities and Public Administration: An Introduction* (pp. 217–235). Edward Elgar.

Dewandre, N., & Ongaro, E. (2022). L'Administration Européenne au défi de la philosophie (et inversement) [The European Administration and the Challenge of Confronting Itself with Philosophy—And Vice Versa], *Revue Française d'Administration Publique*, n.180. [also translated into English and in press as chapter 2 as 'European administration challenged by philosophy (and vice versa)' in Georgakakis, D. (ed.) (2024) *The Changing Topography of EU Administration: Organisations, Actors and Policy Processes*. London: Palgrave.

Drechsler, W. (2025). Ambrogio Lorenzetti's Siena Frescoes and Public Administration Today. In E. Ongaro, G. Orsina, & L. Castellani (Eds.), *The Humanities and Public Administration: An Introduction* (pp. 236–252). Edward Elgar.

Dunleavy, P. (1991). *Democracy, Bureaucracy and Public Choice: Economic Explanations in Political Science*. Harvester Wheatsheaf.

Dunleavy, P., & Hood, C. (1994). From Old Public Administration to New Public Management. *Public Money and Management, 14*(3), 9–16.

Dwivedi, O. P. (1990). Administrative Theology: Dharma of Public Officials. *Indian Journal of Public Administration, 36*(3), 406–419.

Farmer, D.J. (2005). *To Kill the King: Post-Traditional Governance and Bureaucracy*. Armonk, NY: M.E. Sharpe.

Ferlie, E., Lynn, L. E., & Pollitt, C. (Eds.). (2005). *The Oxford Handbook of Public Management*. Oxford University Press.

Floridi, L. (2019). *The Logic of Information: A Theory of Philosophy as Conceptual Design*. Oxford University Press.

Frederickson, H. G. (1980). *The New Public Administration*. University of Alabama Press.

Heath, J. (2020). *The Machinery of Government: Public Administration and the Liberal State*. Oxford University Press.

Huberts, L. (2014). *The Integrity of Governance: What It Is, What We Know, What Is Done, and Where to Go*. Palgrave Macmillan.

Jorgensen, T. B., & Rutgers, M. R. (2015). Public Values: Core or Confusion? Introduction to the Centrality and Puzzlement of Public Values Research. *The American Review of Public Administration, 45*(1), 3–12.

Kasulis, T. (2025). Japanese Philosophy. In E. N. Zalta & U. Nodelman (Eds.), *The Stanford Encyclopedia of Philosophy* (Spring 2025 Edition). https://plato. stanford.edu/archives/spr2025/entries/japanese-philosophy/

Kenny, A. (2010). *A New History of Western Philosophy*. Oxford University Press.

Lynn, L. E., Jr. (2006). *Public Management: Old and New*. Routledge.

Miller, H.T. and Fox, C.J. (2007). Postmodern Public Administration. 2nd revised edition. [Charles J. Fox name appears first in first edition 1996]. Armonk, NY: M.E. Sharpe.

Nagatomo, S. (2025). Japanese Zen Buddhist Philosophy. In E. N. Zalta & U. Nodelman (Eds.), *The Stanford Encyclopedia of Philosophy* (Spring 2025 Edition). https://plato.stanford.edu/archives/fall2024/ent ries/japanese-zen/

Ongaro, E. (2009). *Public Management Reform and Modernization: Trajectories of Administrative Change in Italy, France, Greece, Portugal and Spain*. Edward Elgar.

Ongaro, E. (2013). Explaining Contextual Influences on the Dynamics of Public Management Reforms: Reflections on Some Ways Forward. In C. Pollitt (Ed.), *Context in Public Policy and Management: The Missing Link?* (pp. 192–207). Edward Elgar.

Ongaro, E. (2019). The Teaching of Philosophy for Public Administration Programmes. *Teaching Public Administration, 37*(2), 135–146. https://doi.org/10.1177/0144739419837310

Ongaro, E. (2020). *Philosophy and Public Administration: An Introduction*. Edward Elgar. Available open access [also translated into Chinese, Italian, Portuguese and Spanish] (first edition 2017).

Ongaro, E. (2021). 'Non-Western Philosophies and Public Administration', Guest Editorial. *Asia Pacific Journal of Public Administration, 43*(1), 6–10. https://doi.org/10.1080/23276665.2020.1844027

Ongaro, E. (2022). The Fourfold Nature of Public Administration as Science, Art, Profession, and Humanism: Implications for Teaching. In K. A. Bottom, J. Diamond, P. T. Dunning, & I. C. Elliott (Eds.), *Handbook of Teaching Public Administration* (pp. 26–34). Edward Elgar Publishing. https://doi.org/10.4337/9781800375697.00014

Ongaro, E. (2024). Integrating the Neo Weberian state and Public Value. *International Review of Administrative Sciences, 90*(4), 830–844. https://doi.org/10.1177/00208523241228830

Ongaro, E. (2025). The Arts and Public Administration: How the Consideration of the Nature of Art Can Provide Novel Ways to Understand Public Administration. In E. Ongaro, G. Orsina, & L. Castellani (Eds.), *The Humanities and Public Administration: An Introduction* (pp. 207–216). Edward Elgar.

Ongaro, E. (2026). *Interdisciplinary Approaches and Context Analysis in Public Administration*. Bingley.

Ongaro, E., & Ho, T. K. A. (2025). Eastern and Western Philosophies: Rethinking the Foundations of Public Administration. *Public Policy and Administration, 40*(3), 403–411. https://doi.org/10.1177/09520767251330456

Ongaro, E., Orsina, G., & Castellani, L. (Eds.). (2025a). *The Humanities and Public Administration: An Introduction*. Edward Elgar.

Ongaro, E., Rubalcaba, L., & Solano, E. (2025b). The Ideational Bases of Public Value Co-creation and the Philosophy of Personalism: Why a Relational Conception of Person Matters for Solving Public Problems. *Public Policy and Administration, 40*(3), 429–451.

Ongaro, E., & Tantardini, M. (2023a). *Religion and Public Administration: An Introduction*. Edward Elgar. https://www.e-elgar.com/shop/gbp/religion-and-public-administration-9781800888029.html

Ongaro, E., & Tantardini, M. (2023b). 'Advancing Knowledge in Public Administration: Why Religion Matters', Guest Editorial. *Asia Pacific Journal of Public Administration*. https://doi.org/10.1080/23276665.2022.2155858

Ongaro, E., & Tantardini, M. (2024a). Contours of a Research Programme for the Study of the Relationship of Religion and Public Administration. *Public Policy and Administration, 39*(4), 521–530. https://doi.org/10.1177/095 20767241272897

Ongaro, E., & Tantardini, M. (2024b). Religion, Spirituality, Faith and Public Administration: A Literature Review and Outlook. *Public Policy and Administration, 39*(4), 531–555. https://doi.org/10.1177/09520767221146866

Ongaro, E., & Tantardini, M. (2024c). Bringing Religion into Public Value Theory and Practice: Rationale and Perspectives. *Administration and Society*. https://doi.org/10.1177/00953997241264474

Ongaro, E., & van Thiel, S. (Eds.). (2018). *The Palgrave Handbook of Public Administration and Management in Europe*. Palgrave Macmillan.

Ongaro, E., & Yang, Y. (2024). Integrating Philosophical Perspectives into the Study of Public Administration: The Contribution of Critical Realism to Understanding Public Value. *Public Policy and Administration, 40*(3), 477–496. https://journals.sagepub.com/doi/10.1177/09520767241246654

Ostrom, V. (2008). *The Intellectual Crisis in American Public Administration* (3rd ed.). University of Alabama Press.

Overeem, P. (2025). Socratic Public Administration: The Relevance of Dwight Waldo Today. In E. Ongaro, G. Orsina, & L. Castellani (Eds.), *The Humanities and Public Administration: An Introduction* (pp. 23–35). Edward Elgar.

Parboteeah, K. P., Paik, Y., & Cullen, J. B. (2009). Religious Groups and Work Values: A Focus on Buddhism, Christianity, Hinduism, and Islam. *International Journal of Cross Cultural Management, 9*(1), 51–67.

Perry, J. L., & Christensen, R. K. (2015). *Handbook of Public Administration*. Jossey-Bass.

Pierre, J., & Guy Peters, B. (2000). *Governance, Politics and the State*. Palgrave Macmillan.

Pollitt, C. (Ed.). (2013). *Context in Public Policy and Management: The Missing Link?* Edward Elgar.

Pollitt, C. (2016). *Advanced Introduction to Public Management and Administration*. Edward Elgar Publishing.

Pollitt, C., & Bouckaert, G. (2017). *Public Management Reform. A Comparative Analysis: Into the Age of Austerity* (4th ed.). Oxford University Press.

Raadschelders, J. (2005). Government and Public Administration: The Challenge of Connecting Knowledge. *Administrative Theory & Praxis, 27*(3), 602–627.

Ragin, C. (1987). *The Comparative Method.* Berkeley, CA: University of California Press.

Rosser, C. (2018). Weber's Bequest for European Public Administration. In E. Ongaro & S. van Thiel (Eds.), *The Palgrave Handbook of Public Administration and Management in Europe* (pp. 1011–1029). Palgrave Macmillan.

Rots, A. P. (2016). Reclaiming Public Space: Shinto and Politics in Japan Today. *Proceedings of the International Conference of the Royal Academy for Overseas Sciences—Belgian Institute of Higher Chinese Studies,* 23–45.

Rugge, F. (2013). 'The intransigent context: Glimpses at the history of a problem', pp 44–54. In Christopher Pollitt (ed.) *Context in Public Policy and Management: The missing Link?* Cheltenham, UK and Northampton, MA: Elgar.

Rutgers, M. R. (1998). Paradigm Lost: Crisis as Identity of the Study of Public Administration. *International Review of Administrative Sciences, 64*(4), 553–564.

Shields, P. (1996). 'Pragmatism: Exploring public administration's policy imprint', *Adminisration & Society, 28*(3), 390–411.

Shields, P. (2008). 'Rediscovering the taproot: Is classical pragmatism the route to renew public administration?', *Public Administration Review, 68*(2), 205–221.

Tantardini, M., & Ongaro, E. (2025). The Contribution of the Religious Studies and Theology Literatures to Public Administration: A Review and Outlook. In E. Ongaro, G. Orsina, & L. Castellani (Eds.), *The Humanities and Public Administration: An Introduction* (pp. 152–175). Edward Elgar.

Tooze, A. (2018). *Crashed: How a Decade of Financial Crises Changed the World.* Penguin.

Wagner, C. S., & Raadschelders, J. (2025). From Disciplinary Depth to Interdisciplinary Breadth: The Case of Public Administration. *American Review of Public Administration, 55*(4), 299–317.

Waldo, D. (1948/1984). *The Administrative State: A Study of the Political Theory of American Public Administration* (2nd ed.; first published in 1948). Holmes & Meier and Ronald Press.

Whetsell, T. (2025). Philosophical Pragmatism and the Study of Public Administration. In E. Ongaro, G. Orsina, & L. Castellani (Eds.), *The Humanities and Public Administration: An Introduction* (pp. 50–57). Edward Elgar.

Whetsell, Travis A. & Patricia S. (2011). 'Reconciling the varieties of Pragmatism in Public Administration', *Administration & Society, 43*(4), 474–483

Yung, B. (2014). In What Way Is Confucianism Linked to Public Service Motivation? Philosophical and Classical Insights. *International Journal of Public Administration, 37*(5), 281–287.

CHAPTER 2

Philosophy for Public Administration

Abstract The chapter presents, describes and illustrates the functions that philosophy can perform when applied to public administration (PA). The functions that philosophy applied to a PA problem or theme can perform include: an enlightening function; a critical function; a gap filling function; an integrative function; and a normative function—one or more such functions in a combined way. The discussion of a number of scientific articles in the field of PA that employ and deploy a philosophical perspective as a core part of the argument is used in an illustrative way to highlight the actual performance of these functions in published scholarly work. This chapter articulates the approach in connecting philosophy and PA that we qualify as 'philosophy for PA'. The chapter finally expands on the possibility of combining a range of philosophies to address given PA problems as well as, more ambitiously, to match fields of philosophy with thematic areas of PA as ways of more closely interconnecting philosophy and PA.

Keywords Philosophy · Public administration · Philosophy for public administration · Functions of philosophy for public administration · Approaches to the application of philosophy to public administration

E. Ongaro, *Connecting Philosophy and Public Administration*,
Foundations of Government and Public Administration 1,
https://doi.org/10.1007/978-3-032-01769-7_2

Introduction

This direction of inquiry takes the move from the recognition that philosophy is already there: PA (we use the shorthand 'PA' to encompass the fields of public administration, public management, public governance and government, referring to both the scholarly study and the practice of it—see Chapter 1 for further discussion of definitions and terminology) does have existing guiding assumptions—all intellectual endeavours do (we may not notice them, but they are there)—and therefore mobilising philosophical thinking explicitly enables to address foundational issues in PA.

Analytically, in this chapter, we propose, illustrate and critically review possible 'functions' that the explicit application of philosophical thinking to PA problems can perform. Such functions are introduced and then illustrated through examples of published scholarly works in which one or more philosophical perspectives have been employed to address a PA problem or theme, thereby performing one or more of the functions considered. We finally propose a range of approaches whereby philosophical perspectives can be applied in a combined way to perform the outlined functions, thereby contributing to the investigation of PA problems and topics.

Functions of Philosophy for Public Administration

The *Functions* that the application of philosophy to PA problems can perform can be identified as follows:

- *Enlightening* function: Philosophy sheds light on the guiding assumptions of PA.
- *Critical* function: Philosophy enables to revisit the guiding assumptions of PA, including by identifying possible gaps or outright contradictions in the assumptions that are held, at a given time, in the field of PA.
- *Gap filling* function: Philosophical knowledge can provide constructs and approaches to fill, at least partly, the gaps in PA assumptions, notions and theories.

- *Integrative* function: Philosophy sheds light on the philosophical residue of any social (or other) science applied to PA, and enables or at least facilitates the integration of the multiple disciplinary perspectives that are employed to address public administration problems and themes.
- *Normative* function: Philosophy can provide the rationale for putting forward a normative-prescriptive argument about how the public sector (public governance, public administrative system, public services management) ought to be organised or reorganised.

These functions are considered and discussed in the remainder of this section. Examples of published scholarly works are provided in the next section: they illustrate the usage of one or more philosophical perspectives to examine and discuss a certain PA problem or theme and provide an instantiation and illustration of philosophical knowledge and understanding being used to perform one or more of the functions considered.

Starting from the enlightening function: this is in a sense the most quintessentially philosophical function of philosophy, as philosophy is inherently concerned with the acquisition of rational knowledge and understanding of reality as such, it is the 'science of reason' deployed to understand reality—and reason has been likened to a light, a lamp, enabling human beings to shed light on reality (this is also the root word of the Enlightenment—the cultural-intellectual-philosophical movement that developed in western Europe in the eighteenth century CE). It is also the primal function of philosophy as and when specifically applied to PA: if nothing else, philosophy enables to gain a deeper understanding of a given PA problem or theme by illuminating angles and corners of the problem that are beyond the reach of the social sciences—as a minimum because philosophy, differently from any other science, does not have, nor does it place, borders to its inquiry: it does not set out a defined object on investigation and set of methods to acquire knowledge about it; rather, it is curious about anything and everything and it deploys the power of reason to generate knowledge and understanding in all directions of inquiry.

The critical function is eminently philosophical too. The giant of philosophy Immanuel Kant considered knowledge to be about 'correct' judgements by the reason, where a judgement is a connection of two concepts, one being the noun and one the predicative in a sentence:

what is claimed about the subject of a sentence. Kant then analysed the conditions and limits within which the human reason can formulate judgements, in a major, gargantuan attempts to set out the conditions and limits of human knowledge. Applied to the specific and circumscribed remit of the field of PA, philosophy can provide the conceptual tools for critically revisiting and, if demanded by the outcome of the rational scrutiny, revising the assumptions that guide speculative as well as practical reasoning in public administration.

The gap filling function of philosophy is performed when philosophical knowledge and understanding is employed to address the gaps in extant PA assumptions, notions and theories. For example, assumptions about human motives and behaviours drawn from different social sciences may lead to paradoxical (if not incoherent or outright contradictory) accounts of individual's behaviour (selfish and altruistic, self-determined and hetero-directed, benevolent and malevolent, and so forth) and hence of the dynamics of administrative processes and public decision-making. A philosophical anthropology perspective may then be brought to bear to make sense of such paradoxes (statements that appear self-contradictory and false, and yet may contain a particular kind of truth—see Pollitt & Bouckaert, 2004, p. 163, for a discussion in relation to public administration topics) or outright contradictions, for example by furnishing conceptual tools like the method of the levels of abstraction (Floridi, 2011, chapter 3) whereby, in a nutshell, reality can be studied at different levels, and paradoxes or contradictions may turn out to depend on the levels of abstraction chosen in the inquiry, and be overcome or turn out not to be in contradiction when the appropriate levels of abstraction at which the inquiry unfolds are identified: a task which (only) philosophy can perform. To further corroborate the gap filling function that philosophy applied to PA can perform, we point to the consideration famously been proposed by Waldo that, in the field of PA, theory may be derived not only from empirical evidence actually observed but also and perhaps foremost from philosophical reasoning or imagining about the world (see Overeem, 2025; Waldo, 1984); philosophy can therefore powerfully contribute to the filling of gaps in the highly varied—at times sundry— pool of theories, notions and assumptions that compose the corpus of PA knowledge.

The integrative function of philosophy can be understood as twofold. First, philosophical thinking can provide conceptualisations and intellectual frames that may enable to bridge apparently unconnected or loosely connected theories and concepts drawn from the social (or other) sciences, each social science being apt at investigating its own chosen domain of inquiry, but less so at interconnecting its findings with those of other sciences. Through philosophical framing, therefore, unconnected or loosely connected theories and concepts get to be seen as part of a broader theoretical-interpretive framework. Second, the integrative function arises when philosophy enables to identify and understand the philosophical residue, the philosophical element that remains in any given field of scientific study as the irreducible questions that cannot be addressed within the confines of the specific discipline, with its definite object of inquiry and methods for the generation of knowledge. Since such questions cannot be entirely subsumed into social scientific categories, it is through philosophical thinking that such questions get highlighted and re-interpreted to make sense of them and complement social scientific knowledge. So, for example, economics originally belonged to moral philosophy and then set up home as an independent social science, and indeed one of the most successful social sciences, and at times even a very complacent one (Fourcade et al., 2015), yet its assumptions and concepts periodically require to get revisited, especially at certain intellectual junctures, as underlying questions about human freedom and human motives to act as well as questions about the inextricably multi-level interplay between means and (moral) ends resurface periodically to challenge those assumptions which had become widely held at a certain given period within the economics science. Since PA is an applied interdisciplinary field of study which utilises in a combined way various social science disciplines each with its own specific philosophical residue, and since, furthermore, PA is a field whose specific focus and domain is far from being unproblematically stated and its concepts are far from uncontroversially standardised (Raadschelders, 2005), then we may argue its ties with philosophy are even stronger than for other disciplines like economics, and the unresolved 'philosophical residue' mentioned earlier further gains in prominence, hence philosophical thinking may enable to integrate diverse and possibly differing (when seen within their own level of abstraction and disciplinary field) findings.

Finally, in the most classical 'last but not least', philosophy, or more precisely certain branches of philosophy like morality, ethics and political philosophy, also have an inherently normative thrust, which enables philosophy to also perform a normative function when applied to public administration. Specifically, political philosophy is inherently (albeit not necessarily in all its areas) normative in its thrust: it is about how political institutions (of which administrative systems are a part) *ought to* be set up and operate. We notice the field of PA oscillates between a descriptive/explanatory stance of PA 'as a science' (Ongaro, 2020; Raadscheldes, 2008), and a normative/prescriptive one. This latter manifests itself notably in relation to the discussion of the administrative doctrines: the debate about how the public sector ought to be organised, with successive sets of administrative doctrines, like the New Public Management, New Public Governance, Neo-Weberian State, and so forth, each proposing its own set of recipes to address this inherently normative question (see Chapter 4 for a philosophically informed discussion of the ideational bases of such clusters of administrative doctrines). Political philosophy is key to providing intellectual grounding for PA in its normative stance. It is rarely applied to PA, albeit there are important exceptions, introduced and discussed by Zacka (2022). Ethics, morality and value judgements (axiology) are also central to normative stances in PA (for example, in relation to the dilemmas of street-level bureaucrats, Zacka, 2017). Philosophy, notably through the field of political philosophy and the field of ethics and morality (public ethics and moral philosophy/axiology), can perform a normative function when applied to PA problems and topics, by providing the rationale for putting forward normative-prescriptive arguments about how the public sector ought to be reorganised, and how public services ought to be administered and managed.

This section has aimed at providing an overview of the functions that philosophy can perform for PA. It has done so at an abstract and conceptual level: we now turn to illustrating through specific applications in the literature how such functions can be performed when specific philosophical perspectives, specific philosophies, get applied to address specific PA problems and themes. In the next section, we therefore further illustrate and flesh out our argument through examples of application of philosophy for PA, showing how research work that has applied specific philosophical perspectives to specific PA problems has, implicitly or explicitly, utilised philosophy to perform one or more of the functions outlined here.

EXAMPLES: MOBILISING SELECTED PHILOSOPHIES TO ADDRESS PUBLIC ADMINISTRATION PROBLEMS AND ISSUES

This section presents and discusses a number of worked examples of the functions that philosophy—more specifically: certain selected philosophies and philosophical streams—have been made to perform for application to PA themes and problems. These scholarly works illustrate the range of functions that we have argued philosophy can perform when applied to PA problems. These works have been plucked simply for illustrative purposes, without any pretension of comprehensiveness, as would have been the case, e.g. through systematic literature review; on this point, that is, on the question of how many and how frequently scholarly works in PA rely on scholarly works in philosophy, see the contribution by Tang et al. (2025) which we consider in Chapter 3. An overview of the works is reported in Table 2.1. The selected contributions are discussed in the remainder of this section. They are presented starting from two contributions which address from a philosophical standpoint the topic of the creation of Public Value, a theory in the field of PA which is in many regards deeply entwined with philosophical consideration, to then consider philosophical perspectives that are closely interconnected with the teachings of institutionalised religions, both eastern and western, to finally revisit Hegelian and Weberian philosophy applied to PA, a 'classic' in the field of PA.

The work by Ongaro and Yang (2025) mobilises the philosophy of Critical realism to provide an integrated interpretations of four major conceptions of Public Value, a key notion in public governance and public management, which has itself given rise to an important strand of inquiry and debate. The four conceptions of Public Value are drawn from the work by Hartley et al. (2017), who make a valuable summary of the literature on the topic by distinguishing: (1) a managerially focused concept of creating Public Value that reflects normative agreements of what the public wants (e.g. Moore, 1995, 2013); (2) a policy and societally focused conception of public values as relative citizen consensuses that are detected from constitutions, policies and opinion polls (e.g. Bozeman, 2007, 2019); (3) a psychology-based approach and theory of basic human needs and objectified values (e.g. Meynhardt, 2009); and (4) a process focused approach to study the public sphere in which Public Value outcomes are debated and created (e.g. Benington, 2011).

Table 2.1 Illustrative examples of scholarly applications of philosophical streams to public administration problems and themes

Theme/contribution of philosophy to PA	Reference	Functions performed
Critical Realism and Public Value	Ongaro and Yang (2025)	Enlightening—Critical—Integrative
Personalism and co-creation of Public Value	Ongaro et al. (2025b)	Enlightening—Gap filling—Integrative
Non-violence philosophy and public governance	Baldoli and Radaelli (2022)	Enlightening—Gap filling
Supererogation and Public Value, Public Service Motivation, Administrative reforms	Biancu and Ongaro (2025)	Enlightening—Critical—Gap filling—Integrative
Deliberative mini-publics as Confucian institution and PA	Tong (2025)	Normative
Hegelian philosophy of administration—Weberian 'Proto-Existentialism'	Tijsterman and Overeem (2008)	Critical and Normative

Grounded specifically on Margaret Archer's morphogenetic approach (Archer, 2007, 2012) and the framework of the three overlapping domains of reality wrought out by Bhaskar (1993, 2008)—namely: the Empirical domain, which includes observed events, practices and experiences; the Actual domain, which represents the level at which events (actions) happen; and the Real domain, which includes the underlying causal mechanisms—Ongaro and Yang provide an integrated view of the four conceptions of Public Value, which are seen as unfolding across different phases of the morphogenetic cycle, whereby 'Moore's and Bozeman's approaches treat public values as already objectified and concrete phenomena, the normative consensus at time $= 1$ (T1), that condition and enable agents' reflexive thinking over what they value, which occurs over a period T2–T3, which then leads to a stage (T4) where Meynhardt's approach to public values signals that as a result of agents' reflexivity towards valuing, public values—as structural and cultural elaboration—eventually become pronounced as objectified psychological needs on moral-ethical, political-social, utilitarian-instrumental and hedonistic-aesthetical dimensions. Finally, Benington's insights unpack what is beneath the empirical lived public valuing experiences from the perspectives of structure, culture and agency: it documents and dissects the whole T1-T4 recursive process of Public Value creation, reproduction and transformation that is embedded and informed by the past, agential reflexive evaluation of the present, and their imaginary projective future (Ongaro & Yang, 2025, pp. 8–12 in particular).

The functions performed by philosophy for PA in this scholarly work—the philosophical perspective being in this instance Critical Realism as elaborated in particular by Archer and Bhaskar, and the topic in the field of PA being the creation of Public Value—include both the enlightening function and the integrative function. As regards the enlightening function, in fact, philosophy (and specifically in this instance Critical Realism) provides a novel and comprehensive way to interpret and 'make sense' of social science theories applied to a PA topic: notably, in the specific example, the topic of the creation of Public Value, which has occupied the minds of several PA scholars and innumerable practitioners around the globe. As to the integrative function, whereby apparently unconnected or loosely connected theories and concepts get to be seen as part of a broader theoretical framework, and the philosophical residue, the philosophical element that remains in a given field of study and cannot be entirely subsumed into social scientific categories, gets highlighted and re-interpreted, the chosen philosophical approach of Critical Realism enables to integrate four conceptions of Public Value and to shed light on aspects which are not fully resolved within an exclusively social science based approach. Four theories of PV can therefore be seen in an integrated way by applying Archer's morphogenetic approach: their connections are highlighted through the adoption of a philosophical perspective.

Before moving to the next example of a published work applying philosophy to PA, we may notice that the concept of Public Value is a notion with deep philosophical implications, given its inherent normative dimension as well as its constitutive links with philosophical notions like 'common good' or 'value' and 'valuing'; it therefore represents an area of inquiry in PA—a topical area—which is amply amenable to philosophical treatment, to being analysed from the angle of philosophising. We can therefore briefly sketch a few further lines of inquiry about how a different philosophical perspective may enable to gain understanding of the four main conceptions of PV as delineated above—leaving the full analysis of such perspective of inquiry to another book, to be written by another author. Given the very notion of PV in the contemporary literature originated in the West (it is in many regards a product of western scholarly traditions), it may be intellectually opportune to consider a philosophical perspective from the East, in order to 'challenge' the assumptions of PV theorising that we have been considering so far and expanding the gamut of intellectual facets through which we see the theory and practice of PV (and in this way continuing an emergent strand of scholarly inquiry whose main thrust is the application in a combined way of both eastern and western philosophies to PA problems for enhancing our understanding of the latter; the rationale for this approach is delineated in Ongaro & Ho, 2025, and the special issue 'Eastern and Western Philosophies: Rethinking the Foundations of Public Administration', published as issue 3/2025 in the journal *Public Policy and Administration* and guest-edited by Ho and Ongaro, 2025, provides a first building block in this direction).

We may therefore take the perspective of Confucianism as an eminent philosophical strand which—alongside culture, politics and society—has also permeated the public governance and infused the very conception of the civil servant and the role of the public sector in a number of east Asian countries, and consider how it might be applied to the theory and practice of PV, and with what implications for the very theorisation of PV. Even a very preliminary and tentative initial application of Confucianism reveals the scale of the challenges such perspective may bring about. As a first point, we can start from the very notion of publicness—what is the 'public' in Public Value—and observe that, while modern western philosophy, notably political liberalism from John Locke onwards, frames 'public' and 'private' as antithetical, as contrasting poles, Confucianism rather sees a harmonious public-private continuum (Bai, 2020, chapter 6). This different conception of publicness may have startling implications. Let us consider Meynhardt's psychology-based framework of PV (one of the four conceptions of PV that are mainstream in the literature): from a Confucian perspective, we may question whether Maynhardt's framework (in turn based on the works of western psychologists) may not be able to represent adequately the 'Confucian mind', the psyche as culturally infused by the values and notions and practices and habits of Confucianism, notably in the way in which Confucianism conceives of the relation of the public and the private. Ultimately, the systematic consideration of a psychological, social and cultural Confucian perspective may lead to revising some of the premises of the PV theory, and it may open up novel paths of inquiry about the psychological foundations of PV theory.

As a second point of inquiry, we may query from an eastern perspective the profile of Moore's public manager (another one of the four conceptions of PV that are mainstream in the literature: this was the first conception of Public Value to have been proposed in the contemporary literature, and a conception which is core to PV theory), that is, the conception of the bureaucrat-turned-public entrepreneur who becomes creator of PV. This conception too is framed in western terms and notions, which might get challenged from a Confucian perspective. The figure of the bureaucrat operating as an entrepreneurial public manager creator of PV who has to deal with an authorising environment, which is constituted of the legal framework and the role of elective officials, represents a profile of the bureaucrat steeped into the liberal-western conception of politics and bureaucracy, in which legitimacy stems from 'the people' (government 'by the people') and public decision-making powers are entrusted upon elected officials via electoral representation processes, and only thence bestowed upon tenured officials, thereby implying that bureaucrats must be 'authorised' by elected officials to undertake a given course of action: they must seek authorisation in order to gain the legitimacy to pursue courses of action which aim at creating Public Value. If we revisit this legitimacy and accountability chain from a Confucian perspective, we notice that some key assumptions get turned upside down when seen through this lens. In a Confucian perspective, performing the bureaucratic role inherently requires the adoption of virtuous behaviour (the Confucian notion of rule by virtue/rule by the virtuous), and virtue and morality prevail over law and legalism (this vision has been challenged in the Chinese scholarly debate by Han Fei Zi, an early opponent of Confucianism): in this sense, the notion of 'authorizing environment', within which the public manager operates, takes a very different shape, since a bureaucratic behaviour orientated to creating Public Value is inherently legitimate, it is legitimate per se, so to speak, in a Confucian framework, and virtue-based behaviour prevails over the legal framework, and it is the latter which has to be adapted in case (where there is contrast between the two). Moreover, the Chinese bureaucracy has never operated within an elective system western-style (in this different from other bureaucracies that have also been influenced by Confucian thought, like those of Japan and the Republic of Korea, and which have seen a western constitution foisted upon them after World War II), hence the Chinese bureaucracy has never encountered the dichotomy between the role of the elective and the tenured official—there is no such distinction in contemporary China, nor de facto has there ever been in the history of China. In this regard too, a Confucian perspective brings profound challenges to the consolidated theorisation of PV, and it may open up novel paths of inquiry into the theory and practice of PV, notably in the direction of deeply revisiting the very notion of 'authorising environment'.

As a third point of consideration in examining the challenges brought about by the application of Confucian thinking, we may notice that the reading of PV theory through a Confucian lens may engender a Copernican revolution in relation to 'who' determines what Public Value is. The shift is from 'the public' (however defined) as being centre stage in determining what PV is at a given time and place, to the very bureaucrat taking the podium. Bozeman (2007) wrought out a framework for the detection via multiple channels (statutes, policies, opinion polls and so forth) of what the public values, so that the detection of public values as already objectified and concrete phenomena produces the normative consensus which may guide the public managers in their decisions in order to create Public Value (as we discussed above by applying Critical Realism to PV theory and noticing this is one stage of the PV cycle, indicated at T1). In a Confucian perspective, the core of the process occurs in a meritocratic, top-down, and paternalistic way: the Confucian perspective is one of 'government by the virtuous', in which bureaucrats are at the centre of the stage and make decisions 'for' the public, but not taking direction 'from' the public—it is government for the public, but not from, nor by, the public, albeit consulting the public continues to be a (complementary and ancillary) part of the process of defining what is Public Value. (We may notice the Confucian approach is a perspective which may evoke, for those educated in western philosophy, the Platonic government of and by the philosophers, delineated by the ancient Greek philosopher Plato in his work *The Republic*; Plato's 'common good' approach may have many points of similarity, or at least resonance, with aspects of Confucian thinking; it is instead the liberal theory of the social contract as it arose in the West since the seventeenth century to be in many regards at the antipodes of the Confucian perspective; an audacious attempt to combine liberalism as a political philosophy aiming at protecting universal individual rights while decoupling it from electoral representation and rather harmonising it with Confucianism is developed by Bai (2020), producing an interesting fusion of western and eastern elements, albeit within a firmly eastern-orientated philosophical perspective.)

Finally, with different theoretical underpinnings to Bozeman's approach, we have seen that Benington (2011) evokes the notion of the public sphere as theorised by the (western) philosopher Habermas as central in the process of determining 'what the public values' and hence what is Public Value in a given political community at a given place and time. Here too Confucianism may bring about a Copernican revolution: in fact, in a Confucian perspective it is the (Confucian) sage who assesses what is Public Value in the given historical-political circumstances, with the complementary assumption that in matters of public goods and public services it is the meritocratic bureaucracy to be the venue where sages in such matters (public governance and public services) are to be found; the public sphere (to the extent this very notion may retain its meaningfulness in a Confucian perspective) gets to be shaped under profoundly different premises, centred on the figure of the sage rather than on the larger public (i.e. the totality of the members of the political community). Here too, the adoption of a Confucian perspective leads to querying some of the very premises of the theory and practice of Public Value and it opens up novel avenues of inquiry.

We may now return to the consideration of works published in the extant scholarly literature which explicitly apply strands of philosophy to PA problem. Ongaro et al. (2025b) revisit the philosophy of Personalism and apply it to a connected major PA problem, namely the co-creation of Public Value: the core theoretical preoccupation of this work is to explain the drivers of processes of co-creation, what enables such processes to occur. The authors detect and dissect the lineages existing between key notions elaborated in the philosophical stream of Personalism—these are the notions of common good, active citizenship, relational freedom and intermediate communities—and the notions of, respectively, public value, value co-creation, collaboration and participatory public policy, showing how those philosophical concepts underpin much of the theorising in the co-creation of Public Value literature, albeit their influence is hardly detected and recognised in the extant literature (this gap relative to the absence of a philosophical anthropology underpinning co-creation theorising and the potential of the philosophy of Personalism to fill this gap was first noticed in Torfing et al., 2021). The work by Ongaro et al. (2025b) also aims to make a broader argument, namely, to show how philosophical perspectives can provide ontological grounding in the conception of the human nature and the nature of human freedom for making sense of PA problems (thereby providing a philosophical anthropology for underpinning the theorising of Public Value co-creation—in some regards in line with Isaiah Berlin's theorisation of human freedom).

Specifically, a relational (as opposed to a libertarian) notion of freedom is here found to be able to underpin and make sense of the collaborative processes that enable the co-creation of Public Value, as well as to show some of the roots of the very conception of Public Value in the notion of common good.

This paper performs three of the functions of philosophy for PA that we have outlined. First, the enlightening function, by showing the ideational roots or lineages of the concepts employed in a PA stream of literature: it sets a stream of PA literature within a broader intellectual frame and an ampler, and preceding historically, strand of scholarly literature. It also performs a gap-filling function, in that it joins the dots between observed behaviours leading to co-creation of Public Value (as reported in the findings of social scientific studies on the topic, which also investigate the conditions under which these occur) and the roots of the social agency which is underpinning such behaviours and which is detected in a relational notion of human freedom. Finally, it performs an integrative function in that it may supplement the findings of social psychology studying the motivational structure whereby individuals may engage in collaborative efforts to bring about common solutions to public problems with a philosophical anthropology perspective shedding light on the roots origins of the relationality that underpins the communing amongst persons for the pursuit of forms of common good—a relational conception of human freedom.

A work by Baldoli and Radaelli (2022) draws from another philosophical perspective—indeed, more broadly a stream of thought which embraces ethical, political-philosophical, metaphysical and religious elements—to elaborate a political philosophy with extensive implications for public governance and for public policy and public services management, and especially for PA topics like the co-production of public services and the co-creation of solutions to public problems. This is the perspective of non-violence, most famously brought to the attention of the broader global community by Mahatma Gandhi. In their analysis, Baldoli and Radaelli employ philosophical ideas drawn from the Italian philosopher Capitini, including those of *compresenza* (compresence, referring to 'the connection constructed between all men, both living and dead, at the moment when they present themselves as moral subjects, in contrast with the given reality, and acting as members of an ideal community'—Capitini, 2000, 105—thereby pointing to nonviolent action as the moment in which humans embrace the life cycle overcoming barriers across generations, species, time and epochs, see Capitini, 1998), *liberazione* (liberation, specifically referring to liberation from biological and historical determinism), and *apertura* (intended as openness to others). These ideas are creatively combined and integrated with teachings in the body of wisdom generated over the millennia by the meditation on the Hinduist—as well as Buddhist and Jainist—ideal of *ahimsa*, thereby providing an original and fruitful synthesis between an 'eastern' body of though—Hinduism—and a strand of western philosophy (Ongaro & Ho, 2025; see also Ongaro, 2021; Ongaro & Tantardini, 2023a, 2023b). Baldoli and Radaelli interpret non-violence through the lens of the consent theory of power, whereby governments are assumed to have power only until citizens allow them to exercise this power over them. Re-elaborated this way, non-violence can provide a theoretical lens for working out a bottom-up notion of citizenship, one which may have extensive implications for public policy and administration studies, and notably for capturing some of the political-philosophical underpinnings for theorising notions in PA like that of co-production and co-creation. The main function performed by philosophy for PA in this contribution (in our interpretation) is the normative function: to propose a political theory which, through a different interpretation of citizenship, has also implications for PA themes like those of collaborative governance, co-creation and co-production, and brings to the fore in a normative way a citizen-centric understanding of public governance and the management of public services.

Another perspective, which also intertwines religious and philosophical wisdom, which has been employed in scholarship to shed light on PA themes, is the theological-philosophical perspective of supererogation, whose conceptual contours for application to PA are outlined by Biancu and Ongaro (2025). The notion of supererogation has its roots in Catholic theology and it is used to denote actions which are morally positive yet they are beyond the call of duty, that is, the individual is not required to perform them, nor are they demandable: while they may be perceived as mandatory from a first-person perspective (*i.e.* by the agent at the moment of deliberation), they are not so from a third person perspective (*i.e.* from the point of view of an external observer). The agent feels they have to do what is not required nor demandable to the extent that it is a condition of possibility of liberty and humanity. To further flesh out the implications of the notion of supererogation in more practical terms, consider this passage from Biancu and Ongaro (2025, p. 72):

Let's think of the three pillars of modern politics – liberty, equality, fraternity [...] Liberty and equality are usually considered as required. Protests around the world are always claims for either more liberty or more equality. The State, and therefore PA, must guarantee and protect them. Compared to them, fraternity is usually considered as supererogatory – it is good to have a more fraternal society, but it is not demandable not required. Rather, by contributing to create truly human and free subjects, the supererogatory attitude of fraternity needs to be understood as a condition of possibility of both liberty and equality. When fraternity is missing, freedom and equality are purely formal. Fraternity makes them substantial. Since the liberal state needs citizens who are truly free human subjects, fraternity fulfils those premises on which [...] the liberal State lives without being able to guarantee them by itself

The perspective of supererogation can therefore be seen as a viewpoint from which to interrogate, from a moral philosophy and philosophical anthropology perspective, the key issue of the 'duty' of and in the public service, for both public servants and citizens. Biancu and Ongaro (2025) apply the lens of supererogatory action to critically revisit key theories and notions in PA, such as Public Service Motivation, Public Value management and governance, and administrative reform models. Philosophy in this framework performs both the enlightening function and the critical function, by addressing questions of why public servants should engage in certain actions and adopt certain behaviours at all. Philosophy here might possibly also perform the gap filling and the integrative function: where assumptions of the social sciences about the intentions and behaviours of social agents may appear incomplete or remiss, the philosophical notion of supererogation may fill the gap and lead to a different 'model of man' (model of human behaviour), which may enable to make sense of certain intentionality and behaviour by human beings as social agents in public governance and public management processes.

Another, distinct and distinctive approach in the application of philosophy to public administration is the one suggested by Tong (2025), whose work provides a powerful illustration of the normative function that philosophy, notably political philosophy, can and does perform. Tong (2025) revisits an ancient idea which has roots both in eastern and in western political-philosophical thinking, namely the idea of the random selection from the population of representatives for inclusion in public decision-making processes: the so-called deliberative mini-publics. Tong then elaborates a sophisticated application of this idea to both Confucian political meritocracy (likely the most prominent political philosophical alternative to liberal democracy) and Confucian democracy (a major attempt to combine Confucianism and liberal democracy in the design of public governance). The paper develops this idea and its application specifically by focusing a key public administration problem, namely the selection and promotion of public servants. It delineates how deliberative mini-publics could be introduced and used to improve processes of selection and promotion of public servants, a core public administration and management problem.

Both the critical function and the normative function of philosophy are performed in the work by Tijsterman and Overeem (2008). They revisit the political philosophies of Hegel and Weber in relation to the key issues of public service values and the relationship between bureaucracy (the civil service, the body of civil servants) and freedom. They notice that both differ from the Lockean (John Locke's) political philosophy in that they move beyond an exclusively negative notion of liberty centred on the idea of the need for limiting the power of the state so that the individual may have more freedom. More fundamentally and perhaps also more unexpectedly, they observe that the political philosophies of Hegel and Weber differ widely (also) in relation to the issues of public service values and the relationship between bureaucracy and freedom. Taking the move from highlighting the profound difference between Weber's 'proto-existentialist' notion of freedom (outlined especially in his works on politics and science as profession) and Hegel's view of freedom as anchored in the rational state, whereby the limitations stemming from the obligations set by the law do not hamper personal freedom, rather are the conditions of it, insofar as both subjectively such obligations are accepted with a free will and objectively the political order honours freedom. As summed up by Tijsterman and Overeem (2008, pp. 78–79): 'The point of departure of [Hegel's] dialectical mode of argumentation is the free will, which is the will that wills its own freedom. Starting with this basic principle, and taking the wills of other individual wills into account, Hegel thinks through how social life has to be organised in order to be free. The political order that logically flows from the free will as it enables freedom is the rational state [which] constitutes the framework in which these individual rights can be upheld. Respecting individual rights does not only concern the relation between citizens and government, but requires primarily that individuals of a society mutually recognise each other as persons and consequently take individual rights to be true'. In other words, these values are foremost a predicate of society as a whole; individual rights are embedded in a political culture of which the notion of individual rights is a part[1]' (in interpreting this difference it is worth reminding the reader that both Hegel and Weber accepted the liberal 'negative' freedom of the individual person whose civil, economic and political rights have to be protected by the state).

In summing up Hegel's sophisticated notion of political freedom (and freedom tout court), Tijsterman and Overeem (2008, p. 79) observe that for Hegel: 'Freedom requires that one wills the rational state because only this state makes free life possible. The freedom of the citizens of the rational state has a dual nature; individuals can strive after their own interests *and* have to take into account the interest of the whole and agree with interventions in the name of this. Individuals have private freedom *and* have the freedom of citizens to deliberate about the common good'. Based on the appreciation of the profoundly different notions of freedom in Weber and Hegel, Tijsterman and Overeem draw important conclusions for a key PA topic, namely the conception of bureaucracy. In fact, 'Weber and Hegel conceive of the relationship between bureaucracy and freedom in diametrically opposed ways. While for Weber, bureaucracy poses a threat to liberty, for Hegel this does not have to be the case as the civil service is an essential part of any free state' (Tijsterman & Overeem, 2008, p. 80). It follows that, for Weber, 'every political order entails obligations and coercion, it necessarily limits the possibility to decide autonomously how one is to live. We should not understand Weber's stance only as species of the liberal negative conception of freedom. The point is that every order does not only diminish the free space of individuals to make their choices, but forces people to live heteronomously.

---

[1] Given Hegel's thought has sometimes casually, and deeply wrongly, been associated with forms of totalitarianism, it is worth reporting this passage too by Tijsterman and Overeem (2008, p. 79) about Hegel's conception of individual freedom in its relationship to the state: 'Despite its fundamental character, the rational state does not, according to Hegel, absorb individuals wholly. The customs in which the idea of the state lives do not destroy its subjects' subjectivity; the individual and the modern state do not converge blindly or completely. "In the states of antiquity, the subjective end was entirely identical with the will of the state; in modern times however we expect to have our own view, our own volition, and our own conscience" (para. 261A). Individuals can distance themselves from the political order, be aware of their subjectivity, and from this subjectivity affirm the social order that at the same time underpins them. In order to do so, the individual must go through a process of formation (*Bildung*) that the institutions of social life, such as the family and civil society, offer (para. 270)'.

Every political structure of society predetermines choice and thus cannot be chosen freely, even if one personally agrees with it and would choose it if there was a choice. As a consequence, freedom is a predicate of individuals; the notion of a free society does not make much sense [for Weber]' (Tijsterman & Overeem, 2008, pp. 80–81). In this perspective, individuals can live a non-self-chosen life—and most citizens will do. Some, however, can break this 'iron cage': most likely not bureaucrats, the bearers of the rationalisation process since (according to Weber) 'bureaucratic office offers little or no room for this kind of freedom, being rule-bound and characterized by purpose-rationality' (Tijsterman & Overeem, 2008, p. 81). Rather, it is 'real' politicians who can realise their existentialist freedom 'through autonomous action in the pursuit of self-chosen ends [...] it is the freedom of charismatic political leaders that Weber thought worth protecting. Indeed, for Weber the very "justification for electoral democracy lay in the scope it provided for the individual leader" [...] Now we can see how Weber's advocacy of bureaucracy's subordination to politics flows from his understanding of freedom as existentialist choice' (Tijsterman & Overeem, 2008, p. 81).

Conversely, in Hegel's well-ordered state 'the laws governing social life do not infringe upon freedom but rather make freedom possible, because they are the embodiment of the basic (moral) principles that constitute the political community [..] As a consequence, the civil service (*Regierungsgewalt*) has [for Hegel] a distinctive and prominent role in the constitution of the rational state. This role is twofold. First, the core role of the civil service consists in executing the law by subsuming particular cases under the law [...]. Second, civil servants play an important role in framing new laws, even though they must be deliberated and ultimately voted upon by the legislature and ratified by the sovereign monarch' (Tijsterman & Overeem, 2008, p. 81). This conception has implications also for how the civil service should be recruited and managed: in fact, 'As the civil service identifies with the interests of the state, Hegel calls them the "universal class." This means that, according to Hegel, civil servants have to be lifted out of civil society' (Tijsterman & Overeem, 2008, p. 81). This is a socio-cultural as well as a legal-managerial conception of the bureaucracy which has huge implications about how the civil service ought to function. Equally huge are the implications for how bureaucrats should approach their tasks: 'for Hegel, bureaucratic judgment does not consist in technocratic, rule-bound execution of the law (*technè*), as it does for Weber. Rather, it involves moral deliberation (*phronèsis*) of how a particular case should be subsumed under the public values as expressed in the law. Whereas in Weber's view bureaucratic activity is characterized by purpose rationality, "for Hegel, bureaucracy is *not* a teleological organization with an externally imposed end to implement" (Shaw, 1992, p. 386). Especially in its function of preparing new laws, the civil service has also to engage in moral considerations' (Tijsterman & Overeem, 2008, p. 83); the authors then go on to notice that 'Within Weber's account of bureaucracy, such an understanding of legal and administrative action is impossible. He cannot accept the notion that a political community has a rational idea of how social life should be organized because the good life is beyond the domain of rational argumentation. As part of the process of rationalisation, laws themselves become more and more rational, but they do not have moral worth. The laws are contrary to freedom. As a consequence, bureaucratic values do not flow from the public value of freedom as clearly as in Hegel's state. There is a strong connection between Weber's idea of freedom being under threat in the modern world and the distinctive twist he gives to the idea of bureaucratic neutrality. The bureaucracy should not only serve no particular interests except that of the state, but be subordinated to political leadership as well. This normative requirement is not grounded in the ideals of the liberal democratic state, but in the attempt to save the freedom of political leaders. The other bureaucratic values, however, legality and efficiency, have a different status, as they are intrinsic to the phenomenon of bureaucracy' (Tijsterman & Overeem, 2008, p. 83).

Ultimately, both Hegel's and Weber's conceptions are a normative account of the inner workings of a bureaucracy, they state how the bureaucracy *ought to* function, and why. The bureaucracy as conceived by both scholars upholds the values of legality and efficiency; however, ultimately the role the bureaucracy performs in the political order and in policy-making is profoundly different for Hegel than for Weber, and the distinct roles attributed to the bureaucracy stem from a different notion of freedom. In the work by Tijsterman and Overeem (2008), philosophy (notably the political philosophies of Hegel and Weber) perform both a critical function—in that they enable to revisit the assumptions that guide speculative as well as practical reasoning in the field of public administration about the role of the bureaucracy—and a normative function, as they outline the configuration, functions and workings of the bureaucracy (of public administration) vis à vis the other political institutions and the citizens.

The revisiting of the works of Hegel and Weber also provides connections to two other direction of inquiry outlined in this book: one is the direction of inquiry we qualify as philosophy *of* public administration, as these philosophers delineate the contours of a philosophy of public administration as part of their broader philosophical system (notably Hegel, who outlines in detail a philosophy of PA as part of his broader philosophical system); we return to this perspective in the final chapter of this book (Chapter 5). The second direction of inquiry to which the revisiting of the works of Hegel and Weber contributes is that of *aligning* philosophy and public administration, as Weber's and especially Hegel's conception of the role of the bureaucracy may provide some of the political-philosophical ideational bases for the notion of the Guardian State, and on how to combine it with the Neo-Weberian State (these are discussed in Chapter 4). These directions of inquiry are expounded in subsequent chapters; here, we continue to investigate the perspective of philosophy for public administration, by addressing the question about what broader strategic approaches can be deployed for mobilising philosophy for public administration.

Approaches for Advancing Philosophy for Public Administration

In the preceding section, we have seen examples of scholarly works bridging philosophy and PA. While the very contents of the works considered differed significantly (ranging from Hegelian philosophy applied to the PA topic of freedom and bureaucracy to Critical Realism applied to the theory of Public Value), the basic approach in terms of 'research strategy' employed by these works is similar, in that they all hinge on mobilising one philosophical stream (be it Critical Realism, or Personalism, or Non-violence, or Supererogation, or Hegelian thought, or the ancient political-philosophical idea of deliberative mini-publics) for application to one PA problem or thematic area. They all basically rely on a one-to-one matching between one philosophical stream and one PA topic, whereby the former is plucked for its potential to be applied to the latter (the exception is the work by Tijsterman & Overeem, 2008, which considers and contrasts two philosophies: Hegel's and Weber's).

In this section, we argue that other approaches are also possible and indeed could be even more powerful and fruitful for deploying philosophical thought for application to PA, albeit we immediately recognise they might in practice be much less feasible to implement, especially for reasons of the sheer volume of intellectual and practical resources required of these approaches. This section thus discusses the approach implicit in all the works discussed in the previous section alongside two other possible approaches to mobilising philosophy for PA; the approaches that can be employed for advancing philosophy for PA are presented and discussed. We have labelled such approaches as follows (in italics the driving idea of each approach):

(i) Mobilising *one philosophical stream*
(ii) Mobilising and *combining a range of philosophies*
(iii) *Matching* fields of philosophy with thematic areas of PA.

They are presented in the remainder of this section.

i. Mobilising *One Philosophical Stream*

This is the approach we have seen throughout this chapter. Philosophical streams that have been mobilised in PA scholarly works or that could be mobilised for their apparent potential to address at least some of the key issues in PA include, for example, Positivism, Constructivism, Pragmatism, Critical Realism, Existentialism, Phenomenology, Personalism, Analytical Philosophy, Philosophy of Language and so forth. To mention another example beyond those reported in the previous section, Zhang and He (2020) tackle the PA problem "what makes a public space public?", which is philosophical in nature, and mobilise Ludwig Wittgenstein's language analysis (philosophy of language) to examine and dissect this problem, to then discuss issues and problems of effective public governance, notably in the face of the revolutionary challenges posed by advances in information technologies. When any such philosophical stream gets applied to a given PA problem, the philosophy chosen will perform one or more of the above described functions of philosophy for PA, to a greater or more limited depth and level of problem/type of problematising depending on the PA issue that is being addressed and the 'fit' between the philosophical perspective mobilised and the PA problem object of study. Basically, all the works reviewed in the previous section adopt by and large this approach, with the exception of Tijsterman and Overeem (2008), which adopts approach (ii), albeit to the minimum breadth as the range of philosophies considered numbers two only: the contrast of two opposing—in the view of the authors—philosophical stances, the resulting comparison thus enables to shed light on alternative conceptions of the role of the bureaucracy; this is an efficient research strategy: contrasting two perspectives in order to shed maximum light on the problem under investigation while deploying the minimum possible of intellectual resources compatible with the requirement of adopting more than one philosophical stream; such research strategy greatly advances feasibility, given the huge challenges involved in the mastering of philosophical thinking coupled with the requirement to master the PA problem that is being addressed.

The work by Whetsell (2025) is quite intriguing in regard to the approach of mobilising one philosophical stream for application to PA because of its declared ambition to have found 'the' philosophy most suitable for PA. In discussing the contribution that the philosophy of Pragmatism (broadly conceived, very much in the line of Patricia Shields' elaboration and application to the field of PA) can provide to PA, Whetsell (2025) makes the argument that Pragmatism may represent an almost 'natural fit' for PA, that it may in a sense be the philosophical strand more consonant to the very 'intrinsic features' of PA as both a field of inquiry and a practice. His argument is based on laying out four 'principles' of Pragmatism—namely that Pragmatism is (a) 'practical', (b) 'pluralistic', (c) 'participatory' and (d) 'provisional'—and arguing that such distinctive features or principles correspond to inherent traits of PA as a field. It goes without saying, a number of objections can be raised to this argument: philosophers who work out and dedicate a 'section' of their overall philosophical system to PA, like Hegel, would clearly counter that *it is their very own philosophy to be the natural fit for PA, indeed on the ground (at least in the case of Hegel's philosophy) that their own philosophy is ... the natural fit for the entirety of reality, thence of PA too as a section of it! (We discuss the meaning of Hegel's philosophical system having a section on PA further in Chapter 5.) From the more down to earth perspective of PA scholarship, objections can be raised on multiple grounds about the nature of the PA field and hence towards Pragmatism being 'the' philosophy for PA, rather than just 'one' philosophy for PA, not least for it being so entwined with one country and intellectual context, namely that of the USA. We may further notice that the relatively 'loose' character of Pragmatism—as opposed to, e.g. the more tightly knit and rigid continental European philosophical systems—may in a sense facilitate its 'compatibility' hence applicability to the field of PA. All this being considered, as regards the classificatory approach we outline here, this contribution remains within this first category, namely that of one philosophy for one PA problem—albeit in Whetsell's ambition this one philosophy can, broadly speaking, be applied to the entirety of the field of PA, or at least to vast ranges of the problems and issues of PA.

Summing up, this first approach to philosophy for PA consists in identifying one PA problem and then plucking one philosophy or philosophical stream which appears especially apt to provide the ideational bases to address that PA problem, thereby making philosophy to perform one or more of the functions highlighted above (enlightening, critical, gap filling, integrative, normative). The identification of the PA problem comes first logically, in the sense that at first a PA problem has to be identified, before a philosophical perspective may be mobilised as the 'solution' to shed light on the problem; and it comes first generally also chronologically, although it may also be the case that the philosophical stream that gets mobilised is the 'preferred' philosophy—or one of the preferred philosophies—of the scholar (or practitioner) engaging with the problem, and this represents a case of 'solution in search of a problem'. Given the challenge for a(ny) scholar to master more than one philosophical stream and more than one PA problem, and to do so in such depth to be able to employ the former to tackle the latter, this may very often be the only realistically feasible form that scholarly works connecting philosophy and PA can take.

ii. Mobilising *a Range of Philosophies*, Rather Than 'Just One', and *Combining* Them for Addressing PA Problems

This approach (of which we have seen an exemplar in Tijsterman and Overeem' work, 2008) hinges on combining two or more approaches (often by comparing and contrasting their respective explanatory power) for the investigation of a given PA theme or problem. The key idea here is that by expanding the range of philosophies that are being mobilised, and applying them in a combined way, a better grasp on the PA topic of investigation may be attained. A research strategy similar in thrust is that of connecting the thinking of philosophers to then show the combined influence on PA theory, as in Sager and Rosser (2009) who notice the influence of Hegel on the theorising of the modern bureaucracy of both

Woodrow Wilson and Max Weber, notably in relation to the issue of the politics-administration dichotomy.

A key research and intellectual strategy in this approach can be that of encompassing philosophical perspectives from different intellectual-civilisational traditions. For example, one approach may lie in mobilising and, crucially, combining both eastern and western philosophical perspectives to address PA problems. This approach has been pursued in the special issue in the journal *Public Policy and Administration* guest edited by Ho and Ongaro (2025) which has aimed at revisiting foundational issues in public administration by employing in a combined way both eastern and western philosophies. As a specific example, Yifeng Ni and Ning Liu (2025) combine one eastern and one western philosophical perspective to work out defining issues about the nature of PA as a field of knowledge. Specifically, they mobilise Wang Yangming's interpretation of the Xin Xue school of thought which initiated during the Song Dynasty in China and provided a counterpoint to the then dominant Li Xue school, and William James's philosophy of Pragmatism, for tackling a meta-theoretical issue in PA, namely the theory-practice divide. These two philosophical perspectives are combined to form what Ni and Liu refer to as the 'virtuous-pragmatic approach', whose main thrust is offering a novel and different perspective to tackle the issue of the 'theory-practice' divide in public administration. Their suggested approach is shaped by a combination of these two philosophies, and Ni and Liu's work is therefore illustrative of the combined approach to the application of philosophical thinking to tackle PA problems presented here.

Another work which considers in an interesting way a range of (political) philosophies for PA is Ansell (2025). The paper clearly adopts a normative perspective to the relationship of philosophy to PA. Ansell introduces the notion of 'public philosophy', defined as a system of principles and values that cohere (to some degree) and are invoked and utilised to guide public action and debate, thereby pointing to a normative use of philosophy and to a way to address the 'big question' of what principles and values ought to guide the (re-)configuration of the administrative state (the main reference in Ansell's contribution is PA in the USA, though his theoretical framing of the contribution of philosophy for PA can be applied more widely). The chapter discusses three political philosophies—populism, liberalism and civic republicanism—and contrasts the implications of each of these for the configuration of the public sector: a plurality of philosophical streams are therefore mobilised and their contribution discussed, and in this sense, this contribution falls within the present approach, namely mobilising a range of philosophies and combining them for addressing a given PA problem. At yet another level, Ansell takes a broad perspective in discussing the role of public philosophy (the very term of 'public philosophy' being his coin), almost providing a sort of mapping of how the field of political philosophy can be employed for addressing normative concerns in PA. In this sense, Ansell's contribution can be seen as prefiguring (albeit at bird's-eye view level) the third approach we refer to below—approach (iii)—that of matching entire fields of philosophy (in this case political philosophy) with thematic areas in PA (in this case, the configuration of the administrative state).

We notice that approach (ii)—and even more so approach (iii) discussed below—may require a level of knowledge and expertise—in both manifold philosophical strands and in the field of PA—which may be hard to attain in practice by one scholar only, or even a team of co-authors (albeit not impossible, as the very work by Ni and Liu exemplifies). Such approach may require an important level of cross-disciplinary team-work: the building of networks of teams (teams of philosophers versed in different specific streams, teams of PA scholars focused on different topical areas) working together around common problems, supported by a common framework of analysis.

iii. *Matching* Fields of Philosophy with Thematic Areas of PA

The difference to the previous approaches is that in this approach the thrust is to identify fields/areas of philosophy as privileged intellectual sources for given thematic areas of PA, rather than singling out one specific philosophy for application to a given PA problem. So, for example, political philosophy can be matched to the PA thematic area of 'good governance', or to the PA topic of the issue of the legitimacy of populist elected government vs. the role of civil servants as guardians of liberal democracy (Bauer, 2023; Yesilkagit et al., 2024—we further revisit this topic in Chapter 4 when considering how to align philosophical perspectives and PA doctrines).

Embedded within such broader matching of fields of philosophy to thematic areas of inquiry in PA, it is then possible to apply one or a range of philosophies, individually or in combination (see point (i) and (ii) above), drawn from within the focused field of philosophy, to address

PA problems in the given PA thematic area. Developing approach (iii) can be seen as a longer term—yet highly salient—research programme involving to an even broader extent than approach (ii) a significant level of cross-disciplinary teamwork.

CONCLUSION

This chapter presents, describes and illustrates the functions that philosophy can perform when applied to PA. Philosophy applied to a PA problem or theme can perform: an enlightening function; a critical function; a gap filling function; an integrative function; and a normative function—one or more such functions in a combined way. The discussion of a number of scientific articles in PA that employ and deploy a philosophical perspective as a core part of the argument is used in an illustrative way to highlight the actual performance of these functions in published scholarly work. Most of these articles mobilise one philosophical stream to tackle a chosen PA problem (we have reasons to believe these are representative of the extant literature, that is, that most of the very limited scholarly literature connecting philosophy and PA mobilise one philosophical stream to tackle the chosen PA problem). The chapter therefore expands on the possibility of combining a range of philosophies to address given PA problems, and to, more ambitiously, match fields of philosophy with thematic areas of PA as ways of more closely interconnecting philosophy and PA.

In the next chapter, we turn to another direction of inquiry—which in a sense is the one going the other way around: the direction of inquiry that aims at detecting the extent to which extant scientific works in the field of PA incorporate philosophy into their core argument, with the aim to trace back and 'unveil' the underlying (often implicit) philosophical premises and underpinnings of such works: the direction of inquiry of mapping backwards, from philosophy to PA.

REFERENCES

Ansell, C. (2025). Public Philosophy and the Administrative State. In E. Ongaro, G. Orsina, & L. Castellani (Eds.), *The Humanities and Public Administration: An Introduction* (pp. 36–50). Edward Elgar.

Archer, M. (2007). *Making our way through the world*. Cambridge, UK: Cambridge University Press.

Archer, M. S. (2012). *The Reflexive Imperative*. Cambridge University Press.

Bai, T. (2020). *Against Political Equality: The Confucian Case*. Princeton University Press.

Baldoli, R., & Radaelli, C. M. (2022). Unity in Fragility: Nonviolence and COVID-19. *Italian Political Science Review/Rivista Italiana di Scienza della Politica, 52*(3), 378–390. https://doi.org/10.1017/ipo.2021.38

Bauer, M. W. (2023) Administrative responses to democratic backsliding: when is bureaucratic resistance justified?. *Regulation & Governance, 18*(4), 1104–1117.

Benington, J. (2011). From Private Choice to Public Value? In J. Benington & M. H. Moore (Eds.), *Public Value: Theory and Practice*. Palgrave Macmillan.

Bhaskar, R. (1993) *Dialectic: The Pulse of Freedom*. London, UK: Verso.

Bhaskar, R. (2008). *A realist theory of Science*. 3rd edition. London, UK: Verso.

Biancu, S., & Ongaro, E. (2025). Benevolence, Public Ethics and Public Services: Revisiting Public Value, Public Service Motivation, and Models of Public Administration Through the Ethics of Supererogation. In E. Ongaro, G. Orsina, & L. Castellani (Eds.), *The Humanities and Public Administration: An Introduction* (pp. 68–78). Edward Elgar.

Bozeman, B. (2007). *Public Values and Public Interest: Counterbalancing Economic Individualism*. Georgetown University Press.

Bozeman, B. (2019). Public values: citizens' perspective. *Public Management Review 21*(6): 817–838.

Capitini, A. (1998). *Scritti filosofici e religiosi*. Fondazione Centro Studi Aldo Capitini.

Capitini, A. (2000). A Philosopher of Nonviolence. *Diogenes, 48*, 104–119.

Floridi, L. (2011). *The Philosophy of Information*. Oxford University Press.

Fourcade, M., Ollion, E., & Algan, Y. (2015). The Superiority of Economists. *Journal of Economic Perspectives, 29*(1), 89–114.

Hartley, J., Alford, J., Knies, E., & Scott, D. (2017). Towards an Empirical Research Agenda for Public Value Theory. *Public Management Review, 19*(5), 670–685.

Meynhardt, T. (2009). Public Value Inside: What Is Public Value Creation. *International Journal of Public Administration, 32*, 192–219.

Moore, M. (1995). *Creating Public Value. Strategic Management in Government*. Harvard University Press.

Moore, M. (2013). *Recognizing Public Value*. Harvard University Press.

Ni, Y., & Liu, N. (2025). Bridging the Theory-Practice Divide in Public Administration; A Virtuous Pragmatic Approach of Wang Yangming and William James. *Public Policy and Administration, 40*(3), 452–476.

Ongaro, E. (2020). *Philosophy and Public Administration: An Introduction*. Edward Elgar. Available open access [also translated into Chinese, Italian, Portuguese and Spanish] (first edition 2017).

Ongaro, E. (2021). Non-Western Philosophies and Public Administration, Guest Editorial. *Asia Pacific Journal of Public Administration, 43*(1), 6–10. https://doi.org/10.1080/23276665.2020.1844027

Ongaro, E., & Ho, T. K. A. (2025). Eastern and Western Philosophies: Rethinking the Foundations of Public Administration. *Public Policy and Administration, 40*(3), 403–411. https://doi.org/10.1177/09520767251330456

Ongaro, E., Orsina, G., & Castellani, L. (Eds.). (2025a). *The Humanities and Public Administration: An Introduction.* Edward Elgar.

Ongaro, E., Rubalcaba, L., & Solano, E. (2025b). The Ideational Bases of Public Value Co-creation and the Philosophy of Personalism: Why a Relational Conception of Person Matters for Solving Public Problems. *Public Policy and Administration, 40*(3), 429–451.

Ongaro, E., & Tantardini, M. (2023a). *Religion and Public Administration: An Introduction.* Edward Elgar. https://www.e-elgar.com/shop/gbp/religion-and-public-administration-9781800888029.html

Ongaro, E., & Tantardini, M. (2023b). 'Advancing Knowledge in Public Administration: Why Religion Matters', Guest Editorial. *Asia Pacific Journal of Public Administration.* https://doi.org/10.1080/23276665.2022.2155858

Ongaro, E., & Yang, Y. (2025). Integrating philosophical perspectives into the study of public administration: the contribution of critical realism to understanding public value. *Public Policy and Administration, 40*(3), 477–496. https://journals.sagepub.com/doi/10.1177/09520767241246654

Overeem, P. (2025). Socratic Public Administration: The Relevance of Dwight Waldo Today. In E. Ongaro, G. Orsina, & L. Castellani (Eds.), *The Humanities and Public Administration: An Introduction* (pp. 23–35). Edward Elgar.

Pollitt, C., & Bouckaert, G. (2004). *Public Management Reform: A Comparative Analysis.* Oxford: Oxford University Press.

Raadschelders, J. (2005). Government and Public Administration: The Challenge of Connecting Knowledge. *Administrative Theory & Praxis, 27*(3), 602–627.

Raadschelders, J. (2008). Understanding Government: Four Intellectual Traditions in the Study of Public Administration. *Public Administration, 86*(4), 925–949.

Sager, F., & Rosser, C. (2009). Weber, Wilson, and Hegel: Theories of Modern Bureaucracy. *Public Administration Review, 69*(6), 1136–1147.

Shaw, C. K. Y. (1992). Hegel's Theory of Modern Bureaucracy. *American Political Science Review, 86,* 381–389.

Tang, L., Li, Z., Liu, H., & Jing, Y. (2025). Appraising the Philosophical Influences on Modern Public Administration Research. *Public Policy and Administration, 40*(3), 513–531. https://doi.org/10.1177/09520767241266774

Tijsterman, S. P., & Overeem, P. (2008). Escaping the Iron Cage: Hegel and Weber on Bureaucracy and Freedom. *Administrative Theory & Praxis, 30*(1), 71–91.

Tong, Z. (2025). Deliberative Mini-publics as a Confucian Institution. *Public Policy and Administration, 40*(3), 412–428.

Torfing, J., Ferlie, E., Jukić, T., & Ongaro, E. (2021). A Theoretical Framework for Studying the Co-creation of Innovative Solutions and Public Value. *Policy and Politics, 49*(2), 189–209.

Waldo, D. (1948/1984). *The Administrative State: A Study of the Political Theory of American Public Administration* (2nd ed.; first published in 1948). Holmes & Meier and Ronald Press.

Whetsell, T. (2025). Philosophical Pragmatism and the Study of Public Administration. In E. Ongaro, G. Orsina, & L. Castellani (Eds.), *The Humanities and Public Administration: An Introduction* (pp. 50–57). Edward Elgar.

Yesilkagit, K., Michael Bauer, B., Peters, G., & Pierre, J. (2024). The Guardian State: Strengthening the Public Service Against Democratic Backsliding. *Public Administration Review, 84*(3), 414–425. https://doi.org/10.1111/puar.13808

Zacka, B. (2017). *When the State Meets the Street: Public Service and Moral Agency*. Harvard University Press.

Zacka, B. (2022). Political Theory Rediscovers Public Administration. *Annual Review of Political Science, 25*(1), 21–42.

CHAPTER 3

Mapping Backwards: Underlying Philosophical Bases of Public Administration Scholarly Works

Abstract This chapter explores the direction of inquiry for connecting philosophy and public administration that takes the move from the critical analysis of existing scientific works in the field of public administration, to then detect and trace back the philosophical premises and underpinnings of such works. This direction of inquiry in connecting philosophy and public administration can be called 'backwards mapping'. Three ways in which backwards mapping may be performed are outlined: (i) by having the very authors of the research to make it explicit the philosophical underpinnings of their work; (ii) by having an ex post interpretation performed by a distinct scholar who reviews extant scholarly works with the aim to detect and unveil the underlying philosophical stances and premises of such works; and (iii) by investigating via bibliometric analyses the extant publications in the field of public administration that refer to philosophical scholarly works. Illustrative examples of these three approaches are presented and discussed.

Keywords Philosophy · Public administration · Backwards mapping · Philosophical underpinnings of public administration · Philosophy and public administration

© The Author(s) 2026
E. Ongaro, *Connecting Philosophy and Public Administration*,
Foundations of Government and Public Administration 1,
https://doi.org/10.1007/978-3-032-01769-7_3

OVERVIEW

The direction of inquiry for connecting philosophy and public administration proposed in this chapter takes the move from the critical analysis of existing scientific works in the field of PA (we use the shorthand 'PA' to encompass the fields of public administration, public management, public governance and government, referring to both the scholarly study and the practice of it—see Chapter 1 for further discussion of definitions and terminology), to then trace back and 'unveil' the underlying (often implicit) philosophical premises and underpinnings of such works. It is a form of (ideational) backwards mapping—which provides the rationale for the title of this chapter.

Backwards mapping can occur in at least three possible ways:

- it can be performed by the very authors of the research, who make it explicit the philosophical underpinnings of their work;
- it can be the resultant of an interpretation by other scholars of the philosophical underpinnings of a given PA publication or set of publications; or
- it can be investigated via bibliometric analyses, in order to trace what are the influences on a given PA publication.

The chapter discusses in detail each of these approaches and, based on applications of these approaches, aims to provide an appreciation of how philosophical thinking is being utilised by scholarly works and the extent to which it shapes the field of PA.

ELICITING AWARENESS AND FRAMING THE STANDARDS IN PUBLIC ADMINISTRATION SCHOLARSHIP

The first approach to substantiate backwards mapping from PA scholarly works to their philosophical inspirations and underpinnings entrusts the task of uncovering such underpinnings unto the very PA scholar authoring the work (we remind the reader: it is our assumption that philosophy is always there, in whatever we think or do as human beings, hence there is a philosophical element in any PA argument). Mapping backwards can in fact be performed by the very author(s) of the research, by making it explicit the philosophical underpinnings of their own work. In this perspective, the author 'ought to' feel compelled to consider that disclosing one's own philosophical standpoint (which includes one's own values in an axiological perspective, but it also encompasses issues of ontology, epistemology and political philosophy) is part and parcel of the scholarly work and should see this as a 'standard component' of reporting about the findings of one's own inquiry into the investigated public administration problem or topic. This perspective can be seen as a 'call' to authors to rise to this task, based on a combination of voluntarism and a logic of appropriateness both being at work here. We hear the objection forming in the mind of the reader and we immediately notice that this rarely, or at least somewhat rarely, happens in practice in PA scholarly works (though not so rarely as one might think: see the bibliometric analysis by Tang et al., 2025, on whose findings we report more widely in the section below: 'Mapping the field: bibliometric analyses').

Several reasons can be found for why such 'disclosure' of the philosophical assumptions does not happen quite often in PA scholarship. One reason why this does not happen more often may lie in, very simply, the fact that this is not being expected nor required of a PA publication: a paper or a book can safely navigate all the route from submission to being accepted for publication without incurring any penalisation for not being explicit about its philosophical underpinnings and stance. This aspect is simply not deemed 'important', much less so a 'requirement', so why should an author bother and further complicate one's own argument in the prospective publication, and risk attracting the darts of the reviewers by walking on the slippery terrain of one's philosophical premises, when this is not required, neither formally nor informally? Moreover, making it explicit what the philosophical underpinnings of a piece of research are may not be an easy task, and PA scholars are unlikely to be professionally trained in philosophy, as this is generally not part of the educational curriculum and career paths in this field, hence the hurdle for adding this layer of analysis in the paper may be quite demanding for the very author of the scholarly work. Furthermore, and even more prosaically, we should consider that the limitations to the number of words a paper can contain in many scientific journals and other outlets are such that each and every word should be spent for maximising the chances of the paper 'surviving' the reviewing process: adding another section or even brief para of 'philosophical considerations' is practically highly disincentivised in contemporary PA scholarly conventions.

However, this dire state of affairs ought not to be taken as an immutable given, and initiatives can be taken to raise awareness about the significance of making the philosophical standpoint underpinning a piece of research in PA more explicit (indeed, this is the rationale for and a goal of this book). Setting in motion a process for eliciting more awareness in the PA scholarly and practitioners' community about the significance of engaging with—or at least being explicit about—the philosophical underpinnings of research work may well occur, at different levels. One is the level of the 'epistemological culture', that is, instilling in the culture of the PA scholarly and practitioner community a sensitivity towards this issue, making it more culturally accepted that being explicit about the philosophical underpinnings of one's own work should not be seen as an 'additional task', rather as something that is simply part and parcel of the 'standards' of the scholarly work and the publishing conventions—in a logic of appropriateness framework: institutionalising it as part of the 'rules of the game' of producing research in the field.

Another level at which a process to raise awareness about the significance of making it explicit the philosophical standpoint underpinning a piece of research in PA is that of making this the goal of a deliberate research policy, which can focus on intervening on standards and conventions. For example, a number of PhD programmes in certain departments or schools that 'host' public administration scholarship, like a number of Business Schools in the UK, tend to demand that the philosophy of science (epistemology) adopted by the PhD student be made explicit in their thesis project, and this must occur since the early stages of the doctoral project. This requirement could be expanded in scope to demand that the PhD student considers more broadly the philosophical premises of their work—including, alongside epistemology, the ontological underpinnings or the political-philosophical premises (if pertinent depending on the thematic subject of the thesis project), or the ethical and axiological premises (if pertinent), and so forth. As another example, formats to be adopted in the submission to journals could demand that the submitted contribution not just reports in a dedicated methods section the underlying epistemology, but more broadly asking of authors to report on the underlying ontology, or political philosophy, or axiology as pertinent. In short, there are a number of phases in the knowledge production process on which it would be possible to intervene as part of a deliberate policy to integrate philosophy more systematically into PA.

But while the one depicted so far is a desirable scenario for the future development of the field of PA, for it to connect with philosophical knowledge in order to benefit of it, the question remains: what can be done, here and now, for 'unveiling' the philosophical underpinnings of extant research works and publications in the field of PA? We suggest two main approaches can be delineated to this purpose: an interpretative perspective; and a bibliometric analysis. They are examined in turn in the next two sections.

MAPPING THE FIELD: INTERPRETATIVE PERSPECTIVES

Another approach—to which we refer as 'interpretative perspective'—for unveiling the philosophical underpinnings of extant research works and publications in the field of PA is centred on detecting the philosophical influences on the PA literature as the resultant of an interpretation by other scholars of the philosophical underpinnings of a given PA publication or set of publications. We call this approach as 'interpretative' as it revolves around a second scholar 'interpreting' the work of a given PA scholar in terms of its philosophical underpinnings. It starts from the assumption that only rarely are the philosophical premises of PA works made explicit (see previous section), and hence someone needs to perform this task of 'extrapolating' the philosophical kernel in the extant publications across the PA literature (or at least, given the sheer number of scholarly works in the field, to glean such information out of a selection of the extant publications, seen as particularly significant or representative in some way).

An exemplar of such kind of analysis is Chapter 4 in the work by Riccucci (2010), who discusses the main philosophies of science in use in contemporary public administration (according to Riccucci's interpretation) to then identify major strands of inquiry in an important topic in the field of PA—in Riccucci's analysis, these are works focusing on the topic of representative bureaucracy, a significant area of scholarly interest in PA. Riccucci then classifies extant scholarly works according to the philosophy of science which is (implicitly) adopted by the given strand of inquiry. For each strand of inquiry, Riccucci plucks an exemplar of a PA work particularly representative of that strand of inquiry. So, Riccucci considers that the main philosophies of science in use in the field of contemporary scholarly PA are the following (see Riccucci, 2010, pp. 46–51 for definitions and details): (i) Interpretivism; (ii) Rationalism; (iii) Empiricism; (iv) Positivism; (v) Post-Positivism; and (vi) Postmodernism/Critical Theory. She then delineates the ontology, epistemology and key philosophers for each philosophy of science, as well as the methodology, methods and recording techniques favoured by each of these philosophies of science. Riccucci then delineates the profiles of the strands of inquiry that study the topic of representative bureaucracy from the perspective of each of these philosophies. So, for example, legal studies on affirmative action and case studies on hiring and promotion practices substantiate the strand of inquiry on representative bureaucracy whose premises and underpinnings are in the philosophy of Interpretivism; research challenging the mainstream tenets or suppositions of representative bureaucracy as the chief tool for achieving multiculturalism embody the strand of inquiry on representative bureaucracy whose premises and underpinnings are in the philosophy of Postmodernism/Critical Theory; and so forth. For each strand, Riccucci then identifies a key PA publication which exemplifies the strand. In short, Riccucci's analysis provides an interpretation of the philosophical perspective underpinning each of the main strands of inquiry in the subfield of representative bureaucracy, as an important area of PA inquiry.

Another nice example of an interpretative approach to mapping backwards from a PA work to its philosophical underpinnings is provided by Di Nuoscio (2025), who employs Popper's epistemology to critically analyse a notable public administration work from a philosophical standpoint. Di Nuoscio revisits the key tenets of Popper's philosophy (of science), to then apply it to the 'case study' of scholar Sabino Cassese's analysis of the severe dysfunctions affecting the Italian administrative system, contained in his 'classic' work *Il sistema amministrativo Italiano* (The Italian administrative system—Cassese, 1983). Cassese is a renowned public administration scholar in Italy, and his analysis is a mainstay in the Italian scholarly debate. By utilising the Popperian conceptualisation of the notions of: 'problem', 'causality', 'nomological covering', 'explanation sketch', 'nomological common-sense knowledge', 'primacy of situational analysis' and 'principle of falsifiability/falsification', Di Nuoscio revisits and dissects the core 'components' of Cassese's argument about the dysfunctions of the Italian bureaucracy contained in his book. Di Nuoscio 'breaks down' the components of Cassese's administrative argument by deploying a Popperian framework of analysis and terminology, thereby providing an intriguing application of philosophy to public administration in the logic of backwards mapping.

The contribution by Di Nuoscio sheds light on why and how a philosophical perspective, 'always and necessarily', albeit most often implicitly, underpins any study of public administration, and the contribution that such philosophical analyses can provide by elucidating the philosophical premises underpinning administrative analyses. More in detail, the work by Di Nuoscio discusses at first the rationale for choosing Popper's approach. For Popper (we here follow the structure of the argument as expounded in Di Nuoscio, 2025), problems, rather than 'academic' disciplines, come first: we (human beings) at first encounter a problem. In a Popperian perspective, a problem arises when 'there is a mismatch between an expectation and an observation—which then triggers the quest for new knowledge, which [in turn] arises within the horizon of expectations and the background knowledge of the individual. Observations, in turn, are aimed at solving these problems. An observation without a problem is epistemologically impossible, because without the values, knowledge, and interests of the individual, the world would be reduced to a senseless infinity' (Di Nuoscio, 2025).

The quest for new knowledge capable of addressing and solving an extant problem then triggers the hypothesis generation process which is at the roots of the theory-building and then theory testing process. Most famously, Popper introduced the principle of falsification, whereby a theory can only be deemed to be 'provisionally true', as a single contradictory fact is sufficient to establish its falsity (as Di Nuoscio, 2025, puts it: 'This reveals a logical asymmetry between the confirmation and refutation of a theory: however numerous, confirmations do not establish a theory's truth, whereas a single contradictory fact can, logically, demonstrate its falsity').

We can now turn to illustrating how Di Nuoscio deploys the Popperian conceptual apparatus—notably the notions of 'problem', 'causality' ('immediate' and 'remote' causes), 'nomological covering', 'explanation sketch', 'nomological common-sense knowledge', 'primacy of situational analysis' and (of course) 'principle of falsifiability', as defined within Popper's philosophy—to vet the structure of the argument of Cassese's (1983) study of the Italian administrative system (in his analysis, Di Nuoscio also assumes a principle of utility maximisation by individuals as rational actors, which he derives mostly from the works of Ludwig von Mises, and whose philosophical roots can be associated to the works of Jeremy Bentham and James and John Stuart Mill). Starting with the *problem* that Cassese identifies, this is framed in the terms of what he calls the 'endemic dysfunctions plaguing the Italian state administration' across key public functions and policy sectors, described through qualifications like the 'deterioration' and 'devaluation of public functions', the 'difficulty in formulating and executing unified policies' (policy coordination), and the 'lengthening and slowing down of procedures'(inadequate response times to deliver public services—see Cassese, 1983, pp. 283–285).

To explain such dysfunctions, Cassese looks for *causality*, seeking to trace a causal chain starting from the immediate causes and extending back to more remote ones. Chief amongst the *immediate causes* is the lack of clear attribution of public functions to public offices, with resulting overlapping and intersecting functions, due to single tasks being split amongst multiple offices, as a main cause of the identified dysfunctions (Cassese, 1993, p. 274). To make sense of these dysfunctions, Cassese applies certain nomological rules (which Di Nuoscio, resorting to Popper's analytics, collectively qualifies as *nomological covering number one*), which 'can be made explicit as follows: (i) "The greater the number of actors involved, the harder it becomes to reach coherent decisions"; (ii) "As the number of decision-makers increases, so does the time required to make decisions"; (iii) "The less clearly competencies are defined among parties, the more overlaps, conflicts and uncertainties arise in action strategies". These 'covering laws' provide the necessary framework for Cassese to select causally relevant facts from countless possibilities, enabling him to pinpoint the specific factors underlying the dysfunctions in Italian public administration that he aims to explain' (Di Nuoscio, 2025).

Cassese's analysis then shifts to what Di Nuoscio qualifies as the *remote causes*, of which the immediate ones are, in turn, effects. These remote causes are sought in the administrative action of three entities: (a) the Parliament, which by treating administrative organisation as an area of secondary interest had de facto forfeited its responsibility to shape the organisational function of the Public Administration (Cassese, 1983, p. 279) and ultimately countenanced an opaque and ineffective organisational structure for the Italian public sector; (b) the Government, which also has forfeited its responsibility in effecting a coherent administrative reform policy (Cassese, 1983, p. 280); and (c) the administrative staff, and here Cassese deploys an argument much in line with the arguments developed by Niskanen (1973) and Dunleavy (1991)—albeit with a very different terminology and a different reference discipline, as Niskanen an d Dunleavy resort to economics as the reference disciplinary perspective and proceed in a deductive way, while Cassese mostly resorts to administrative law, with some elements of the sociology of organisations, and frames his insights as 'rules of experience'. The argument lies in attributing a bureau-shaping behaviour to the tenured officials (the bureaucrats), ultimately resulting in the dysfunctions identified as the problem. The analysis of these remote causes is also developed by working out certain nomological rules (*nomological covering number two*). And '[T]his causal imputation also relies on implicit "rules of experience." Causes (a) and (b) are identified through the following nomological insights: "whoever regards something as secondary will not give it special attention" and "without coordination of decisions, a coherent solution to a problem is unachievable". Cause (c), on the other hand, presupposes the principle: "in the absence of a party asserting a shared public interest, particularistic interests will dominate"' (Di Nuoscio, 2025).

Di Nuoscio then further notices that Cassese's theorisation serves as an *explanation sketch*, that is, an argument in which the underlying 'covering laws' that explain the phenomenon are left implicit. The identification of immediate and remote causes rather occurs through 'nomological common-sense knowledge' (Weber, 1903/2012, p. 5), which, as Di Nuoscio notices, is 'described by Popper as "a-problematic" and "trivial"[and] Although methodologically secondary, this nomological underpinning is logically essential for constructing the explanatory hypothesis, as without it, the identification of causal relations would be impossible' (Di Nuoscio, 2025, relying also on Di Nuoscio, 2003, pp.18ff).

Reliance on rules of experience brings with it notable challenges, though. The nomological covers identified this way may apply to a range of instances, but not to others. Rules such as 'without coordination of decisions, a coherent solution to a problem is unachievable' have been disproved (falsified) in a number of instances, as human history can provide plenty of evidence to the contrary (we can echo here Simon's point about the proverbs of administration, Simon, 1946). However, such 'rules' may be found to fit the specific circumstances under analysis (revealing their ad hoc nature). This can be referred to through the notion of the *primacy of situational analysis*. Faced with the potential for multiple explanations compatible with the situation to be explained, the researcher can only rely on what Popper calls 'situational analysis': the most precise possible reconstruction of the unique interweaving of typical aspects that, in the view of the researcher, constitutes the causal context generating the explanandum. A detailed situational analysis allows the researcher to progressively reduce the number of alternative explanations that, while compatible with the explanandum, are incompatible with each other (Di Nuoscio, 2018), which is what Cassese does in his analysis here reported. In particular, Cassese applies a logic of utility maximisation to public employees, and he assumes that those who advanced the interests of public employees (including the trade unions) acted rationally from their viewpoint as utility maximisers by exploiting the favourable circumstance represented by the void left by parliament and governmental (non-) action.

Finally, as an outcome of his analysis, Cassese comes out with a theory about the causes of the administrative dysfunctions of the Italian administrative system (at least as it used to work in the early 1980s, when the analysis was developed). Such 'theory' can be submitted to the Popperian *principle of falsifiability*. In fact, Di Nuoscio observes:

> Cassese's proposal is an example of a theory that can be subjected to falsificationist criticism. The following two types of propositions can be empirically tested: i) those describing the explanandum: "the disqualification and deterioration [of functions], the high degree of interdependence of structures and the consequent difficulties in formulating and executing unitary policies, the constitution of coordinating bodies, the general lengthening and slowing down of procedures" (Cassese, 1993, p. 278) and ii) those describing the "initial conditions" – e.g. "norms with no apparent relationship, coming from heteroclite periods and sources, slide over each other and suddenly become immobilized in an organizational architecture whose design cannot be discerned"(Cassese, 1993, p. 279), "only the organization of five ministries is defined in general organizational acts of a normative nature [...] The organization of the other apparatus is regulated by multiple acts, codes and ministerial decrees that are added to each other in a disordered manner [..] As is evident, we are faced with empirically testable propositions, which may be contradicted by contrary facts (potential falsifiers) that, if identified by the scientific community, would lead to the falsification of the theory, thereby creating the conditions for the formulation of a new hypothesis that incorporates the new empirical evidence.(Di Nuoscio, 2025)

In sum, by providing a range of concepts and the terminology and then the application to the specific case example, in order to compare the underlying epistemological premises of Cassese's administrative argument about the Italian administrative system with the underlying premises of alternative administrative arguments, Di Nuoscio (2025) aims at furnishing a more general method and framework of analysis that enables to 'extrapolate' the underlying epistemological premises of PA scholarly works and compare the underlying structure of their arguments. The contribution by Di Nuoscio can therefore be seen as aimed at providing a framework and method for vetting the structure of administrative arguments as developed in the PA literature, to then compare them through a common conceptualisation and terminology in order to facilitate the establishment of a common ground for the critical discussion of administrative arguments (a similar thrust—but without any explicit reference to philosophy as the underlying discipline—can be found in Barzelay, 2001). Such framework as proposed by Di Nuoscio is based on a philosophical framing and a philosophical terminology, and it can therefore substantiate a structured approach to mapping backwards from a public administration work to its philosophical underpinnings and premises.

The main thrust of Di Nuoscio's account is working out the philosophical premises of a PA work, and it is therefore fitting that it is being presented in this chapter dedicated to backwards mapping. At the same time, Di Nuoscio also aims at introducing more systematically Popper's epistemology into PA studies, by working out a framework to be used for analysing and comparing PA studies, and in this sense, his work can also be seen as another example of mobilising philosophy for PA, which we have discussed widely in the dedicated Chapter 2 centred on the approach of 'philosophy for public administration' (specifically, in Di Nuoscio's contribution, philosophy performs two of the functions characterising its application to PA problems: the enlightening function as well as the critical function).

In concluding this section, we notice that the interpretative approach—which we have here seen applied mainly through the lens of the branch of epistemology—could be expanded to other areas of philosophy beyond epistemology.

Mapping the Field: Bibliometric Analyses

Philosophical influences on the PA literature can also be investigated via a different approach and method, namely through bibliometric analysis. In their work, Tang et al. (2025) scout the Web of Science database, one of the largest databases of scientific works (published in journal article format), to detect references to works that have been published in philosophy journals that are contained in all the PA journal articles that have been published during the period of observation.

Tang et al. (2025) have thus identified 58,633 PA journal articles published in the period from 1900 to 2022 (only original research articles and review articles were included), and their associated 2,246,146 references. During the same period, WoS indexed 563,237 philosophy journal articles (in the WoS journal categories of 'philosophy' or 'ethics'). After checking for duplicates, they matched the 2,246,146 PA references against the 563,237 philosophy journal articles and obtained 3,548 PA journal articles (out of 58,633) influenced by philosophy, in the sense that they cite at least one article published in a philosophy journal (books or other outlets are not considered in the database).

Interestingly, while the above datum indicates that on average ca. 7% of PA articles cite (at least one) philosophy article, the authors detected a growing trend: while PA articles in the 1970s tended to very limitedly cite philosophy journals (only 0.9% of PA articles did so in 1970), a much larger share of ca. 14% of PA journal articles cite at least one article published in a philosophy journal in 2022. As the authors point out (Tang et al., 2025), this datum may point to an enhanced 'absorption of philosophical knowledge' into the field of PA, an upwards trend. Through additional investigation, the authors also find that PA research in the 1970s tended to cite books, government documents and other types of references that are not journal articles, while more recently published articles in the field of PA tend to cite other journal articles: this trend might therefore be seen as part of a 'scientization' of the PA field which—at least for research published in the form of journal article—tends to cite other journal articles, possibly seen as more 'scientific' than the grey literature which tended to be cited in the 1970s. To reiterate, there is evidence that over time PA journal articles more and more cite other journal articles rather than works published in other formats, which can explain the upwards trend of philosophy articles being cited by PA articles, as part of a general trend to PA articles more and more often citing other articles.

However, it is by far not a given—it is indeed quite surprising (positively surprising, from the viewpoint of this book aimed at bridging the fields of philosophy and PA)—that PA journal articles tend to cite more and more philosophy articles—better: that there are more and more PA articles referencing at least one philosophy article, both in absolute value and as a share of the total PA articles that are published every year. This is even more striking when zooming in on the trend over time: in fact, the authors found, 1.4% of PA journal articles published over the period 1970–1999 cited philosophy articles (at least one philosophy article); 4.5% of PA articles published over the period 2000–2010 cite philosophy articles, and 11.3% of PA articles published over the period 2011–2022 cite philosophy articles, with a 'striking' ca. 14% of PA articles citing philosophy articles in the year 2022 (the last year for which this analysis was carried out). To further reinforce the contrast, in the period before 1970, that is (given the temporal scope of the WoS database), from the year 1900 to 1969, out of the 3,717 PA research articles that were published, merely four articles (four!) cite philosophy studies.

To better appreciate this evidence, Tang et al. (2025) also examine the number of PA journal articles citing articles from the 'typical' disciplinary fields underpinning PA studies, namely political science, economics, law and management (see, e.g., Rosenbloom et al., 2022). Not unexpectedly, PA journals tend to reference more often from these disciplines (next to referencing other PA journal articles, which represent the most cited category of articles) than from philosophy articles: in decreasing order, PA journal articles cite first of all other PA journal articles (over 90% of PA journal articles cite, not unexpectedly, at least one other PA journal article), then political science articles, then economics articles, then management articles, then law articles and finally philosophy articles. Therefore, while the 'common wisdom' appreciation that PA articles tend to tap knowledge from the other social sciences articles (and first and foremost, amongst the social sciences, from the 'big four' of political science, economics, management and law), and that PA articles tap knowledge first of all from previously published PA articles (as commonsensical), it is intriguing to notice that philosophical knowledge seems to have been on the rise as a source of reference in PA scholarly works published in the form of journal articles.

The authors then further analyse in which PA journals the most articles citing philosophy articles can be detected; not unexpectedly, the journal *Science and Public Policy* tops the ranking, with *Public Administration Review, Public Management Review* and *Administration and Society* as the next journals hosting the larger number of PA articles citing philosophy articles. They then examine which are the philosophy journals hosting the most philosophy articles being cited by articles published in PA journals; here too not unexpectedly philosophy and ethics journals concerned with the social sciences represent the primary sources: *Journal of Business Ethics* tops the ranking, with 'purer' philosophy journals like *Philosophy and Public affairs* and *Journal of Political Philosophy* ranking in seventh and eight position respectively. This finding suggests that the share of PA articles drawing on philosophical knowledge *stricto*sensu may be (much) smaller than PA journals drawing from philosophical knowledge *lato*sensu, which includes the fields of ethics and the philosophy of science.

Another interesting finding provided by Tang et al. is that PA journal articles citing philosophy articles tend to garner more citations than PA articles not citing philosophy articles. This may be due to a number of reasons—and possibly this can be due simply to the fact that PA articles referencing philosophy articles are likely to touch on topics that elicit more interest from other researchers for the very subject they investigate. However, it is intriguing to consider that works that do draw from philosophy as one of their intellectual sources of knowledge and understanding of reality tend to be better positioned to also win the coveted prize (in the scholarly world) of attracting more citations!

Yet another finding by Tang et al. concerns the topics that are more frequently examined by PA articles which cite philosophical references contrasted with the topics of PA articles which do not cite philosophy articles: 'wicked problems' as well as problems pertaining to research and innovation top the ranking of PA articles which also draw from philosophy articles, while (interestingly) climate related issues top the ranking as the subject of PA articles which do not cite philosophy articles.

Before concluding this section, it is worth recalling a limitation of the work by Tang et al. (2025), work which provides an impressive and highly valuable and useful contribution for the purpose of connecting philosophy and PA. In fact, the bibliometric analysis carried out by Tang and Colleagues encompasses journal articles only, thereby leaving out works published in other formats. In the case of philosophy, the book format has historically been a privileged outlet for communication of the 'findings' of philosophical inquiry; this is especially so in the case of the 'classics' in philosophy, their work being often published in book format, but also contemporary philosophy prizes the book format to an extent that is not (anymore) appreciated in the social sciences (the book format used to be central also in PA studies in the past, but the trend to privilege journal articles, also driven by academic career patterns modeled on other social sciences like economics, has led to disparaging the book format in PA studies, unfortunately).

Summing up, the work by Tang et al. (2025) sheds light on the extent to which philosophical knowledge is 'absorbed' in PA scholarly works. While their findings point to philosophical studies being less drawn upon than the social sciences in PA studies (not unexpectedly), they find, however, that tapping philosophical knowledge may be on the rise: it may be growing over time. They also show that the field of ethics may be the philosophical area most tapped in PA (again, not unexpectedly, given the significance of the topic of public ethics and related areas like anti-corruption and integrity of governance), thereby corroborating and underpinning with empirical evidence what may have been 'common wisdom' in this regard, yet previously undemonstrated.

More broadly, at the 'meta-analysis' level, the study by Tang et al. can be seen as path-making: it can open a path of inquiry which has in bibliometric methods the approach to survey and map the multiple interconnections between the fields of philosophy and PA respectively. Bibliometric approaches can enable to walk the road connecting these two fields of scholarly inquiry (a two-way road: not only PA tapping philosophical knowledge but also the other way around), for mutual benefit.

CONCLUSION

This chapter has explored the direction of inquiry for connecting philosophy and public administration that takes the move from the critical analysis of extant scientific works in the field of public administration, to then detect and trace back the philosophical premises and underpinnings of such works. We refer to this direction of inquiry as 'backwards mapping', because it moves from extant PA works 'back' to their philosophical ideational sources.

We propose and outline three ways in which backwards mapping may be performed: (i) by the very authors of the PA research, who make it explicit the philosophical underpinnings of their own work; (ii) by an ex post interpretation by a distinct scholar, who reviews extant PA scholarly works with the aim to detect and unveil the underlying philosophical stances and premises of such works; and (iii) by investigation via bibliometric analyses, of which there are many techniques and variants, with different specific foci and units of analysis—a powerful example of one such analysis being the study by Tang et al. (2025), who have looked into the references cited by the journal articles published in PA journals over the period 1900–2022.

Overall, these three suggested approaches may provide valuable tools to raise awareness of the philosophical underpinnings of PA scholarly work, both retrospectively by investigating extant publications in the field of PA and tracing their philosophical premises, and prospectively by eliciting self-awareness as PA scholarship develops and traverses the challenging seas of the theory and practice of public governance and public administration worldwide.

REFERENCES

Barzelay, M. (2001). *The New Public Management. Improving Research and Policy Dialogue.* University of California Press.

Cassese, S. (1983) *Il sistema amministrativo italiano,* Bologna: Il Mulino.

Cassese, S. (1993). *Il sistema amministrativo italiano.* il Mulino.

Dunleavy, P. (1991). *Democracy, Bureaucracy and Public Choice: Economic Explanations in Political Science.* Harvester Wheatsheaf.

Di Nuoscio, E. (2003). *Methodological Individualism, Scientific Explanation, and Hermeneutics.* In N. Bulle & F. Di Iorio (Eds.), *The Palgrave Handbook of Methodological Individualism.* Palgrave.

Di Nuoscio, E. (2018). *The Logic of Explanation in the Social Sciences.* Bardwell Press.

Di Nuoscio, E. (2025). Epistemology and Public Administration: A Trial-and-Error Approach. In E. Ongaro, C. Barbati, F. Di Mascio, F. Longo, & A. Natalini (Eds.), *Public Administration in Italy: The Science and the Profession.* Palgrave.

Niskanen, W. A. (1973). *Bureaucracy: Servant or Master.* Institute of Economic Affairs.

Riccucci, N. (2010). *Public Administration: Traditions of Inquiry and Philosophies of Knowledge.* Georgetown University Press.

Rosenbloom, D. H., Cravchuk, R. S., & R. M. Clerkin (2022). *Public Administration: Understanding Management, Politics and Law in the Public Sector* (9th ed.). Rutledge.

Simon, H. (1946). The Proverbs of Administration. *Public Administration Review, 6*(1, Winter), 53–67.

Tang, L., Li, Z., Liu, H., & Jing, Y. (2025). Appraising the Philosophical Influences on Modern Public Administration Research. *Public Policy and Administration, 40*(3), 513–531. https://doi.org/10.1177/095207672412 66774

Weber, M. (1903–1906/2012). *Roscher and Knies and the Logical Problems of Historical Economics* (1903–1906). In H. Henrik Bruun & S. Whimster (Eds.), *Max Weber. Collected Methodological Writings.* Routledge.

CHAPTER 4

Aligning Philosophical Perspectives and Public Administration: Ideational Public Governance Configurations

Abstract The core argument of this chapter is that a fuller understanding of administrative doctrines benefits from considering their ideational bases. Administrative doctrines can be defined as elements of knowledge with a prescriptive/normative thrust about how public administration ought to be organised. Examples of administrative doctrines include: the New Public Management; New Public Governance and Collaborative Governance; the Neo-Weberian State; Public Value governance and management; the Guardian State: and not least the base case of 'Old Public Administration'. We employ the notion of ideational public governance configuration to indicate the overall configuration of administrative doctrines and the ontological, epistemological, linguistic, ethical-moral and political-philosophical ideas which enable to conceptualise, understand, interpret and explain administrative doctrines. The notion of ideational public governance configuration is therefore a conceptual tool to mobilise philosophical thinking for unpacking and elucidating the ideational bases of our understanding of public administration.

Keywords Philosophy · Public administration · Administrative doctrines · Public sector reform · Ideational public governance configuration

E. Ongaro, *Connecting Philosophy and Public Administration*,
Foundations of Government and Public Administration 1,
https://doi.org/10.1007/978-3-032-01769-7_4

INTRODUCTION AND RATIONALE

This chapter explores a distinct direction of inquiry in connecting philosophy and public administration, namely, it addresses the issue of the alignment between administrative doctrines and their ideational bases. Administrative doctrines or public administration doctrines (hereafter referred to simply as 'PADS') are defined as elements of knowledge with a prescriptive-normative thrust about how public administration ought to be organised. Thus, 'Old Public Administration' and 'New Public management' (Barzelay, 2001; Dunleavy & Hood, 1994; Hood, 1991) are both seen in this perspective as sets of administrative doctrines, as are 'Collaborative Governance' and the 'New Public Governance' (Osborne, 2006); the 'Neo-Weberian State' (Pollitt & Bouckaert, 2017); 'New Public Administration' (Frederickson, 1980) and 'New Public Service' (Denhardt & Denhardt, 2015); 'Digital-Era Governance' (Dunleavy et al., 2006); 'Public Value Governance and Management' (Alford & O'Flynn, 2009; Benington, 2015; Benington & Moore, 2011; Bozeman, 2007; Bryson et al., 2015; Hartley et al., 2017; Meynhardt, 2009; Moore, 1995)—to mention some of the most prominent sets of administrative doctrines in an illustrative, but far from being exhaustive, fashion. Tons of ink have been poured about these reform doctrines, yet analyses of the philosophical underpinnings of such doctrines are less copious.

The contribution this chapter aims to make is providing an original and distinctive entry point to the study and practice of public administration doctrines. Our argument is that a fuller understanding of PADS benefits of considering their *ideational bases*, and that such ideational bases encompass ontological, epistemological, linguistic, ethical and political-philosophical perspectives. Ideational bases shape both the conceptual context of knowledge of PADS—that is, how scholars understand PADS: the underlying premises which ground scholarly work of knowledge generation in PADS—and the factual context of knowledge of PADS—that is, the beliefs systems and assumptions (as mental anticipations and perceptions) which shape the collective understandings of the ways in which public administrations operate and public policies occur. Understanding context is key to any progress and development of comparative public administration and public management (Pollitt, 2013): it is therefore argued that a systematic consideration of the ideational bases of administrative doctrines is a lynchpin for the theory of public administration, to which this book ultimately aims to contribute, through the analysis of the connections between philosophical thought and public administration doctrines (the significance of mobilising philosophical thinking for bettering and refining our understanding of context in public administration is further discussed in Ongaro, 2026).

A better understanding of PADS demands that administrative doctrines are appreciated in the light of considerations of ontology, epistemology, semiology, values (axiology) and ethics, and political philosophy. We suggest that the label of *ideational public governance configuration* may be employed to indicate the overall configuration of a given set of administrative doctrines together with the ontological, epistemological, linguistic, ethical-moral, and political-philosophical ideas which enable to conceptualise, underpin, interpret and explain such administrative doctrines.

This chapter, therefore, aims at complementing the substantive state-of-art knowledge about PADS that the social sciences provide by delineating the contours of the ideational public governance configurations which enable a deeper understanding of administrative doctrines, by resorting to broader branches of knowledge, rooted in philosophical thought and cognate fields in the humanities. We conceive of ideational public governance configurations as combinations of foundational ideas about ontology, epistemology, semiology, ethics and morality, and political philosophy that enable an understanding of PADS in their broader ideational context. Philosophical thinking is therefore used broadly in this approach, and philosophy performs in general terms all the functions identified when applied to PA—enlightenment, critical, gap filling, integrative, normative—with an emphasis on the normative function, given philosophy in this framework enables and supports the broader and better understanding of the ideational bases of administrative doctrines, namely ideas which are inherently normative in thrust.

Two qualifications are required. First, ideational public governance configurations are multiple—that is, different ontological, epistemological, linguistic, ethical and axiological, political-philosophical positions and stances that align with given conceptions of how the public sector ought to be organised are possible. However, not all configurations are consistent; therefore, there will be only a limited, albeit potentially ample, number of configurations which are internally consistent and 'make sense', that is, that are not internally contradictory. For example, a Marxist political philosophy will presuppose an ontology of dialectical becoming, a usage of language emphasising transformation and change process (using the gerundial form to highlight the inherent becoming of reality), and an ethics which places social class centre stage; any treatment of public policy and administration from a Marxist ideational public governance configuration will therefore require some extent of consistency with such ontological, epistemological, political-philosophical, ethical and linguistic assumptions. In other words, only a limited set of configurations are consistent (that is, certain administrative doctrines presuppose certain philosophical ideas). The framework of the ideational public governance configuration is used as conceptual tool to revisit the extent to which a given set of administrative doctrines [PADS-10] presupposes certain ideational contents (which we label through nine categories, as [1–9]), ultimately enabling the search for consistency,[1] through a dynamic, continuous process of alignment.

The second qualification is that the scholarly study of different configurations presupposes the adoption of a perspective of uncommitted ontology: that is to say, that the observer (the public administration scholar investigating administrative systems, the practitioner making administrative systems work) remains uncommitted about the actual existence of the entities that are being considered, in fact, '[W]hile committed ontology is concerned with the existence of those entities it discerns, uncommitted ontology remains agnostic about their existence' and '[U]ncommitted ontology focuses instead on the elucidation of the ontological presuppositions or assumptions of a particular author, theory or community' (Al-Amoudi & O'Mahoney, 2016, p. 16). In order to be able to critically analyse and appreciate different ideational public governance configurations, beholders have to 'relinquish' their own ontological beliefs (and related assumptions in the other domains of philosophical speculation) and assume an agnostic stance, which enables a dialogue amongst different perspectives.

Finally, it may be pointed out that the notion of ideational public governance configuration complements and completes a range of other notions widely employed in the field of PA and that are amenable to

---

[1] Consilience is another term which might be employed here: Wilson (1998) introduced the term 'consilience' to indicate the linking of knowledge generated across disciplines to achieve common ground for explanations: ideational public governance configurations represent a framework to try and attain consilience across forms of knowledge in relation to administrative doctrines.

philosophical inquiry and appreciation: these notions are those of 'practice', 'model', 'paradigm', ideal-type' and 'utopia'—all notions that are of central importance for PA (Achten et al., 2016; Bouckaert, 2020a; Ongaro, 2020, chapter 8).

IDEATIONAL PUBLIC GOVERNANCE CONFIGURATION: ANALYTICAL FRAMEWORK AND BUILDING BLOCKS

The analytical framework employed to illustrate what an ideational public governance configuration is hinges around the notion of ideational alignment with administrative doctrines of an array of forms of knowledge and understanding which originate in nine main theoretical-disciplinary perspectives (see Fig. 4.1 for an illustration). Of these theoretical-disciplinary perspectives, four pertain to dimensions of ontology [indicated as ONTO-1 to ONTO-4]; two of political philosophy and theory [POLPHIL-8 and POLPHIL-9], the others pertain to epistemology [EPI-5], language analysis [LANG-6], ethics, morality and axiology [E-7]. They represent macro-areas of human knowledge, intended in the broadest sense and encompassing varied forms of knowledge, wisdom and understanding in the investigation of reality. They pertain to philosophy and philosophical thought, broadly intended, and its application to various realms of problems and research and policy questions: they represent philosophical perspectives to the study and practice of PADS (Ongaro, 2021, 2022a).

This analytical framework is intended for use both by the 'detached beholders', the scholars observing and studying administrative and public policy phenomena from the outside, and the 'engaged practitioners', the decision-makers aiming at changing with the purpose of improving (in some sense, and given their very own values, which are part and parcel of the ideational bases they use to frame administrative phenomena for purposes of action) the functioning of administrative systems. We are of course aware that both these profiles—the pure scholar and the engaged practitioner—are somewhat fictional, as most of the people in real flesh and bones involved in public policy and the functioning of administrative systems will be somewhere in-between the pure scholar and the engaged practitioner, but the message we intend to convey is that we consider the notion of ideational public governance configuration and the analytical framework to describe it that we introduce in this chapter to represent a useful conceptual tool both for theory-development and scholarship

> Ontology
>   o   Reality in itself / what there is / Being and nature of things [ONTO-1]
>   o   Conception of time and space/place [ONTO-2]
>   o   Conception and understanding of human nature: the self / identity / model of man-human being [ONTO-3]
>   o   Configuration and nature of society: social ontology - social structures and individual agency [ONTO-4]
> Epistemology and Logic: what we can know, how we can know [EPI-5]
> Language and discourse analysis: nouns (entities) or gerundial (becoming/process) [LANG-6]
> Ethics – values/axiology: public ethics / public values / integrity of public governance [E-7]
> Political Philosophy:
>   o   Perspectives and approaches to the issue of the legitimacy of the political system and public governance [POLPHIL-8]
>   o   Constitutional-political doctrines and conceptions of State and Citizen: Constitutional Liberalism and Liberal-democracy (Representative Democracy; Deliberative Democracy; Participatory Democracy); Libertarian Liberalism; Socialism (Social-Democracy); Communism-Marxism (Leninism, Maoism); Conservatism; Republicanism; Radical Democracy (Follett); Direct Democracy; New Authoritarianism – Fascism; Absolutism; Confucian Meritocracy; Confucian Democracy; ... [POLPHIL-9]

ALIGN WITH

❖ Administrative Doctrines [PADS or PADS-10], such as: Old Public Administration; New Public Management; New Public Governance and Collaborative governance; New Public Service; New Public Administration; Digital Era Governance; Neo-Weberian State; Public Value Governance and Management; ...

Fig. 4.1 Ideational public governance configuration: key components and alignment

(thereby encompassing both research and education and the teaching of philosophy for public administration, Ongaro, 2019, 2020—chapter 9— and 2022b) and for praxis and practice-orientated purposes. In short, both academics and practitioners will benefit of it, we think.

The basic framework of analysis of the ideational public governance configuration, outlining the ideational alignment of such areas of knowledge with administrative doctrines, is illustrated in Fig. 4.1.

The components of the framework are succinctly discussed in the remainder of this section. A number of 'actual' sets of administrative doctrines and the corresponding ideational public governance configurations are proposed and critically reviewed in the next section, in an illustrative way, in order to show how the notion of ideational public governance configuration can be utilised in the field of public administration.

Given space limitations, this chapter can only provide a bird's-eye view, done in an evocative manner by way of just listing and labelling such huge areas of intellectual inquiry and very briefly hinting to their main traits, and we refer the readers to the pertinent literature for any in-depth study they wish to pursue further (so the reader interested in the issue of the legitimacy of a political system and public governance will have to delve into the corresponding political philosophy literature; the reader interested in issues of public ethics will have to develop into the ethics literature and public ethics specifically, and so forth). In other words, these areas of intellection or ideational dimensions can only be evoked and labelled here, leaving it to the reader to unpack each of them depending on the intellectual-practical set of circumstances in which they are embedded, that is, the given 'here-and-now' of the concrete and specific administrative system they are studying or contributing to making it work (the two functions of studying and making something work not being necessarily mutually exclusive, rather intertwined).

The first four dimensions point to the significance of ontology for any field of study, and therefore also for PADS (Ongaro, 2020, chapter 4): these four dimensions bring to the fore the question of the nature of reality as such, and of the 'essence' of the entities that are being investigated. The labels ONTO-1 'Reality in itself' and ONTO-2 'Time and space-place' point to the significance of the ontological premises for any investigation into any specific field of reality: What is the nature of reality? Is it about being or becoming? Do entities exist in themselves or in relation to something else/ the other? What is time, are there different notions of time, what do these notions entail, and which one(s) should we employ for understanding and for changing the world and society? What is space and how does it shape the conditions for humans to think of entities and interact with them, and what is a 'place' and how does it shape social structures, social practices and social agency? The answers provided to these, and many other related fundamental questions shape any aspect of the way in which we understand and act upon social realities. Each student or practitioner of PADS will study and practise it by relying on their ontological views, that is, their vision of the world (often referred to with the German-language term of *Weltanschauung*, which has become technical terminology to express this concept), which is shaped by their answers (whether explicit or implicit) to the questions above.

Two other sets of set of fundamental questions derive from, and interconnect with, the aforementioned dimensions, and they too are ontological in nature. The first set of questions concern the conceptions and understanding of human nature (the branch of philosophy sometimes referred to as the investigation of Soul and Mind): Who are we? How do we understand the nature of human beings and the meaning of 'being human'? How do we understand the 'self' and the 'other'? what 'model of man (human being) do we assume, and what does it mean in terms of understanding human behaviour and individual freedom, the motivations driving individual agency, their underlying logics? Such questions are closely connected to questions of ethics and morality (how to live well?) and of political philosophy (how to live well together?), but they can also be seen as a set of distinct questions and issues, more ontological in nature, which we label in our framework as ONTO-3 'Conception and understanding of human nature'.

The other set of questions—also ontological—concern the nature of 'social entities', that is, the very entities we are most interested in when studying society (public administration being part and parcel of society). Questions about the nature of social entities constitute our fourth dimension, which we have labelled: ONTO-4 'Configuration and nature of society'. The field of social ontology has only relatively recently acquired wider currency and become an area of active inquiry (at least in comparison with the ontological questions we have previously discussed, which have occupied the minds of philosophers over the millennia). Social ontology is a specialised field of ontology which is concerned with the nature and foundations of social entities, with 'the study of what sort of things exist in the social world and how they relate to each other' (Elder-Vass, 2010, p. 4). Some of its roots can be traced in the work of Émile Durkheim, who introduced the notion of a 'social fact' and the question of under what conditions a fact is 'social', most famously through his work on the causes leading certain individuals at certain moments of their life to commit suicide: by demonstrating the influence of social conditions on even such most individual act which is the decision of taking one's own life, Durkheim uncovered the 'reality' of social facts and their influence—that is, their causal power—on individuals' lives. Such entities like social groups, social conventions, customs and habits of a society, social norms, institutions and organisations, social practices, social processes and social structure can all be defined as 'social entities' and form the object of inquiry of social ontology, as a regional ontology, an ontology focused on a specific 'region' of reality. Administrative systems and public policies partake of society and can be seen as instances of social entities, and as such they benefit from the findings of social ontology, and any under-standing of administrative systems and public policies is also underpinned in social ontology (Ongaro, 2020, pp. 133–138). Social ontology can therefore contribute to shed light on the foundations of our knowledge of PADS.

But how can we gain knowledge of reality and its entities? What can we know? These and similar questions constitute another set of fundamental philosophical questions which give rise to epistemology: the branch of philosophy which aims at ascertaining what we (human beings) can know, and how—in other words: what is 'rigorous' knowledge, that is, knowl-edge that is grounded and that is 'certain'. These questions are at the roots of the modern sciences, and therefore also of the social sciences, and are relatively more frequently discussed in social scientific research works than ontological questions usually are, notably in relation to issues of 'adequacy' of the research methods employed (e.g. Howell, 2012). Linked to this area of philosophy as well as to the next one (hence also operating as a bridge between the two) is the field of Logic. We refer to this fifth dimension of the ideational public governance configuration with the label EPI-5 'Epistemology'.

Language is key to human beings and to our possibility of thinking of reality and our own self. Language can for example reveal whether we think of reality in terms of entities (possibly revealed by the emphasis on the use of nouns rather than gerundial to describe reality) or as process and becoming (revealed by the use of the gerundial rather than nouns in the description of reality). An important philosophical strand, the analytic movement, spearheaded by scholars like Bertrand Russell and Ludwig Wittgenstein in the first half of the twentieth century and especially influ-ential in the Anglosphere and the English-speaking world, emphasises the analysis of language as key to any process of generation of knowledge which can uphold the highest standards of being rigorous. The related fields of semiology (the study of signs—the relationship of a meaning to a signifier—and of symbols) and linguistics (the scientific study of language) represent major theoretical-disciplinary perspectives whose significance for the field of PADS can hardly be overestimated. We label this sixth ideational dimension—philosophy of language and its related fields—as LANG-6 'Language and Discourse Analysis'.

Ethics—our seventh area, labelled E-7 'Ethics'—is another key philosophical-disciplinary perspective which is central to PADS. It also concerns issues of values in human decisions and behaviour, an area of philosophical inquiry also known as axiology. In public life broadly and PADS specifically these profiles are considered by such fields of research and practice as public ethics and integrity of governance, and all those scholars investigating public values. These are an integral part and active areas of inquiry in the field of PADS (e.g. Chapman, 2003; de Graaf et al., 2016).

Political philosophy can contribute in many ways to shedding light on key issues in PADS. A first area we highlight here is the issue of the legitimacy of public governance. Legitimacy concerns the political-philosophical question of what justifies a political order and makes it just, thereby 'giving reasons' to its members to value it (Bird, 2006). Legitimacy is therefore concerned with gaining the consent of the members on the very foundation of the polity under consideration and, relatedly, with being able to command loyalty to the political system from its participants (Ongaro, 2020, p. 162). A key issue for the comparative study of PADS is whether the issue of legitimacy applies only to the political system as an indivisible whole (an example would be the claim that a liberal-democratic regime is legitimate per se, an authoritarian system is not), or whether we may consider that specific public governance and administrative arrangements within the political system can be analytically distinguished (i.e. focused for purpose of study and analysis), and it is therefore possible to analyse the legitimacy specifically of the public administrative system, or selected areas of it (like its policing service, or its public healthcare services, or its educational system, and the like), while 'bracketing' the issue of whether the broader political system per se may be deemed to be legitimate or not (Ongaro, 2020, pp. 183–184 in particular). Zacka (2022) has pointed out the rediscovery of the issue of the legitimacy of public administration as such, the articulation of standards of good government as distinct from good public policy, as a central endeavour for political philosophy applied to public administration. Legitimacy is foundational to public governance, and therefore, this represents a first major ideational area in which political philosophy contributes to PADS. We label this POLPHIL-8 'Perspectives and approaches to legitimacy of the political system and public governance and administration'.

Another way in which PADS is linked to political theory relates to the constitutional doctrines which provide the ideational underpinnings and foundations for a political system and hence its administration and public policies. We label this POLPHIL-9 'Constitutional and political doctrines'. The history of humankind has seen a range of political regimes, and notably since the eighteenth century CE onwards the problem of the constitutional foundation of a political system (which intertwines with the issue of its legitimacy recalled earlier) has been tackled by a variety of doctrines. By way of hinting to these, we can mention the following political doctrines: Constitutional Liberalism and Liberal-democracy (which combines Constitutional Liberalism with Representative Democracy—a treatment of the topic of bureaucracy in the framework of Liberal-democracy has recently been provided by Heath, 2020), and, as 'variants' or 'expansions and complements' of it, Deliberative Democracy (centred on the notion of the public sphere and the analysis of the conditions for democratic deliberation processes to occur in the public sphere) and Participatory Democracy (centred on citizen participation to political-public decision-making processes); Republicanism (hinging on the core tenet of civic participation); Conservatism (emphasising tradition and a preference for preserving extant institutions as the default option); Libertarian Liberalism (centred on a radical individualism); Socialism (Social-Democracy: combining Liberal Democracy with an emphasis on welfare and attenuating social and economic inequalities); Communism (with its varied strands including Marxism *stricto sensu*, Gramscian thinking, Leninism, Maoism); Radical Democracy (centred on small self-governing communities, *àla* Mary Parker Follett); Direct Democracy (emphasising direct decision-making, including through referendums and other means of consultation of 'the people'); New Authoritarianism—Fascism (emphasising natural social hierarchy and strong, centralised, unchecked leadership); Absolutism (emphasising the prerogative of the absolute sovereign—be it an individual person or a group—which gets to concentrate all authority whereby 'what the sovereign commands as law is law'); and so on. All these doctrines refer to the constitution and foundations of a political system, of which the administrative system is a constitutive component enabling its functioning. The incorporation of the study of constitutional and political doctrines into analyses of the functioning of PADS represents therefore a major contribution for the analysis of the ideational underpinnings of PADS.

Finally, our object of primary investigation and core concern (the 'dependent variable') is the administrative doctrines that shape the 'model' of public administration and management in a given jurisdiction, i.e. how the public sector 'ought to' be organised. We refer to these doctrines collectively as 'Administrative Doctrines', and as part of the ideational public governance configuration they figure as its tenth element, therefore labelled: PADS-10.

IDEATIONAL PUBLIC GOVERNANCE CONFIGURATION OF THE NEW PUBLIC MANAGEMENT, NEW PUBLIC GOVERNANCE, THE NEO-WEBERIAN STATE AND THE GUARDIAN STATE

This section develops an application of the ideational public governance configuration approach to a range of administrative doctrines which have over time become quite popular in the academic and practitioners' discourse about how to reconfigure public administration. What follows is a brief and very much bird's-eye overview of administrative doctrines with the purpose of illustrating how to apply the approach of the ideational public governance configurations. A more in-depth overview and critical review would require a comprehensive literature analysis which, alongside being almost impossible to undertake as a solo effort, it would also occupy an entire volume on its own, and it is therefore beyond the scope of this book chapter. If, however, such an analysis or range of interconnected analyses of administrative doctrines were to be elicited by this work, it would be a most welcome outcome that this book aims to bring about.

The more limited goal of this section is simply to furnish some introductory armchair reflections about the form that public governance ideational configurations may take. This is, as mentioned, a bird's-eye view which focuses very high-level, abstract and, indeed, under-specified sets of doctrines, captured here in their more general terms. More well-specified doctrines are better amenable to being analysed in relation to their specific ideational bases. However, PADS which are commonly debated in the field of public administration are quite often under-specified—often, though not always, evoked in rather vague and underdetermined fashion—hence the analysis of ideational bases can only correspondingly be schematic, stylised and highly simplified rather than articulate, fleshed-out in the details and nuances, and in-depth.

The remainder of this section examines the ideational public governance configurations of the following administrative doctrines: New Public Management; New Public Governance and Collaborative Governance; Neo-Weberian State and Public Value; and the recently introduced Guardian State. Others could (and indeed should) have been examined, but reasons of limited space (and also the very rationale for this section, which is to be illustrative, definitely not exhaustive, in showing how to apply the construct of ideational public governance configuration) require to limit the sets of PADS being considered in this section. Preliminarily, we outline the contours of the ideational public governance configuration of the so-called Old Public Administration.

An Ideational Public Governance Configuration of Old Public Administration

The idea of an 'old' public administration, a sort of *ancient regime*, a relatively stable and uncontested state of affairs about how public administration ought to be configured and the public sector be run is mostly fictional. Yet it can be a useful fiction a suitable starting point for our narrative[2] to assume that, before the reforms of the public sector started, roughly, in the 1980s with the New Public Management and followed by successive reform waves inspired by different doctrines, there was a time when public administration was configured (at least at the ideational level, if possibly not factually) roughly along the lines of a Weberian bureaucracy set up to administer a growing welfare state, and that this model of public administration was either actually implemented, typically in the western part of the world (with distinctive twists depending on the history and context of the given country/jurisdiction), or anyway this was the model to which to tend to. In a number of respects, in fact, working under the assumption that the Weberian state is the starting point in relation to which all PADS have been developed, either by reaction (e.g. the NPM), or by evolution (e.g. the Neo-Weberian State, which deliberately and explicitly picks up key traits of the Weberian administration) contains more than a grain of truth and it may provide an apt entry point for our analysis.

---

[2] Simplistic or outright wrong as this assumption may be: that is, lumping all non-western countries together under the label of 'developing countries' and, on their way to development, assuming they had to mimic western countries in all respects—like capitalist economy and liberal democracy—and that this process also included adopting 'western-global public' administration as their model of reference for how the public sector should be organised. This is obviously a simplistic or plain wrong storyline (or a discussion, see Drechsler, 2020), but such narrative has wielded huge influence in the past and can in this sense be utilised as a useful starting point.

What are then the underlying ideational bases of Old Public Administration? Starting with the constitutional-political doctrines (POLPHIL-9), we can say that most constitutional-political doctrines are in principle compatible with a (stylised) Weberian public administration; however, not all of them are: direct democracy, for example, is hardly compatible with OPA.

As to the issue of the legitimacy of public administration (POLPHIL-8), doctrines underpinning OPA assume that legitimacy of public administration is a given and it is hardly in question. Indeed, most of the doctrines which emerged since the 1980s are a response to a (real or perceived) loss of legitimacy of the public sector, variously depicted (rightly or wrongly) as inefficient, inadequate, wasteful, unresponsive and so forth—a rhetoric that, on the rise since the 1980s, has transformed the technical term of 'bureaucracy' and the derivative 'bureaucratic' into a word with a negative connotation in the eyes of the public at large (although the reference to bureaucracy in a derogatory term very much pre-dates the 1980s, this and the next decade saw a rise of an anti-bureaucracy rhetoric in public discourse and common parlance). Doctrines of reform of public administration (like the ones we discuss in the next sub-sections) have been promoted and propounded as ways for the public sector to recover an allegedly lost legitimacy in the eyes of the public—so their narratives went on. Reform narratives have pinned their pretension to regain legitimacy for the public sector by making it 'work better and cost less' on a range of political-philosophical premises: the philosophy of utilitarianism can be seen to lie at the roots of many of the claims of the NPM (Ongaro, 2020, pp. 177–179); Platonic 'common good' arguments can be interpreted as lying at the roots of Public Value governance and management doctrines (not by chance a critique to PV theory has come in the forms of criticism to conceiving of public managers as 'Platonic guardians', see Rhodes & Wanna, 2007 and 2008, and for a rejoinder, Alford, 2008); at times palingenetic views have been propounded to mark the revolutionary character of digital governance; and so forth. Doctrines about OPA, on the contrary, are quite silent on the issue of the legitimacy of public administration: they rather assume it as a given. Perhaps, if a theory of legitimacy is at all adopted in OPA, it is a Hegelian one, whereby the state, and its public administration, is legitimate in its own right: it is a pure and simple necessity, something that necessarily is and does not need to justify its existence and functioning (provided the state is the rational state which is the condition of individual freedom and is predicated on it, see chapter 2).

Likewise, the public ethics (E-7) philosophical stance underpinning OPA can be interpreted as centred on a rather unproblematic assumption about public servants and citizens fulfilling their respective duties, in relation to the workings of public organisations and citizen-public administration interactions. The citizen is a user of public services with no special or additional roles to perform other than complying with the regulation set up to administer the public services. The citizen in this perspective is not yet a 'customer', a 'co-producer', a 'co-creator' and so forth, as envisaged by later successive waves of PADS—it does not perform multiple roles: the citizen simply uses public services, and does so in compliance with the way in which they are administered to her/ him.

As to the language of OPA, it is likely to be articulated in nouns rather than verbs (LANG-6): to be centred on entities that make up the configuration of the public sector and the citizen-public administration interactions. The use of the gerundial to describe the functioning of public administration in terms of processes, suggesting transformation and dynamism, rather concerns PADS that emerged later on, often in contrast to OPA, which is a set of doctrines implicitly suggesting stability rather than movement or change, a language of entities (the term entity deriving from the Latin *ens*, which means 'to be', the things that are, that exist) rather than processes (which would entail a language of becoming, rather than one of being).

A realist epistemology (EPI-5) whereby things—which exist outside of the subject knowing them—can be known with some degree of certainty and 'objectivity' can be seen as the default and unproblematised epistemological stance here. Likewise, the underpinning social ontology (ONTO-4) can be assumed by default to be a realist one.

As regards assumptions about human nature (ONTO-3), these— not problematised, at least in our fictional, stylised depiction of OPA doctrines—hinge around a robust sense of responsibilities and obligations informing public servants discharging their duties, and citizens complying with theirs. No special traits driving people to strive to maximise one's own utility, like in NPM's depictions of public servants and citizens; or to perform heroically beyond the assigned duties to rise to the call of co-producing public services or co-creating solutions to public problems, like in the New Public Governance, are predicated of the social actors active in OPA. Individual agency and social structures/structural conditioning are not especially problematised in this perspective.

Finally, a Newtonian-Galilean conception of time and space (ONTO-2) is likely to underpin OPA: the problematics of simultaneity being brought about by the information revolution and more explicitly considered by, e.g. the PADS of Digital Era Governance (Dunleavy et al., 2006) or other sets of doctrines, are, almost by definition, not part of OPA. Finally, a traditional 'realist' ontology (things—a mind-independent reality of some sort—exist in themselves 'out there', at least to some extent irrespective of the knowing subject), centred on entities rather than processes, may be assumed as default ontology in OPA (ONTO-1), reflected in the entity-oriented language we have already seen—although ontological issues are likely not problematised in this set of doctrines, and OPA may be compatible with a wide range of ontologies (it does not require specific ontological commitments, or those can be minimal at most).

An ideational Public Governance Configuration of the New Public Management

The NPM is a (loose) set of administrative doctrines which has been dissected from multiple angles, at least since the seminal article by Hood (1991). Effectively summed up as 'Specialisation plus Incentivisation plus Marketisation' in another seminal paper (Dunleavy & Hood, 1994), it has its theoretical roots in the strand of economic theory of the Public Choice (whose roots are in Downs, 1965, and developments in Dunleavy, 1991 and Niskanen, 1973, 1994) coupled with a vaguely defined aspiration of 'business-like government', driven by the alleged superiority of the management methods and techniques in vogue in the private sector.

Its ideological inspiration has been associated to Neo-Liberalism (Roberts, 2011), hence it makes sense to look for its inspirational political doctrines (POLPHIL-9) in this stream of thought first of all. Neo-Liberalism is a set of political doctrines predicated on rolling back the state and placing an emphasis on limiting state regulation of economic activities. It seems to be closely connected to an earlier strand of thought: the Libertarian strand of Liberalism, which may be especially fit for the NPM, given its emphasis on consumer choice, a negative conception of freedom centred on removing obstacles to expand the range of options available to a self-determining individual. In short, while the NPM is compatible with a highly varied range of constitutional-political doctrines, Libertarian Liberalism seems to be especially dovetailing a number of key features of the NPM.

From the perspective of the advocates of the NPM (a dwindling cohort nowadays than during its heyday in the 1990s), the very legitimacy of the state gets questioned, and the legitimacy of the public sector can only be restored of it can deliver 'value for money' (POLPHIL-8). While the notion of value for money has been used in a technical sense as a declension of cost-benefit analysis of public programmes—'Value for Money' was indeed the name given to a UK government framework to assess prospective public programmes and projects—the underlying ideational basis is one in which the state and the public sector are hardly legitimate per se, rather it is what and how they deliver—the outputs and outcomes of public programmes—or indeed at times what they do not deliver— the rolling back of the state in order to reduce the taxpayers' burden —that provides legitimacy to public action (a radical critique of the legitimacy argument implicitly aligned to the NPM has been developed by Cordelli, 2020, who has criticised the 'privatised state', namely the state systematically contracting out the running of key public functions like the management of prisons, or welfare offices, or security and warfare—which can be seen as a possible product of a form of application of NPM administrative doctrines—as fundamentally lacking legitimacy, at least from a liberal constitutionalist standpoint). Public sector legitimacy within the NPM is meant as being always conditional on the level of performance of the public sector: hetero determined rather than intrinsic.

It may be problematic and highly controversial to align a public ethics philosophy (E-7) to the NPM. Some works have considered the NPM to be detrimental to the public service ethos, to be potentially harmful and lead to a depletion of ethical behaviour, due to its emphasis on incentives, market-type competition-oriented rewards and other mechanisms leveraging extrinsic motivation drivers. At the same time, it may be argued a strong public ethics to be assumed in the NPM, exactly to ensure that the very emphasis on incentives, competition and so forth—all centred on the logic of reward and utility maximisation—do not lead the public system morally adrift. Not just the public servant but the citizen-customer as well is assumed to enter utility-maximising and satisfaction-maximising logics and mechanisms, while at the same time refraining from gaming the system to her/his own advantage. A robust ethics of duties seems to be assumed in NPM doctrines, without it being nurtured by the system. Utilitarianism and sense of duty are assumed to, somehow, simply co-exist.

As to language and discourse (LANG-6) underpinning this set of doctrines, NPM doctrines may be more closely aligned to a rhetoric of process and action: verbs conjugated in the gerundial form rather than nouns. Underlying epistemologies (EPI-5) may be varied; Neo-Positivism, with its influence on factual knowledge and verifiable propositions, can be ideationally closely aligned to NPM.

In terms of social ontology (ONTO-4), NPM doctrines can be more easily aligned to methodological individualism, with its emphasis on explaining social facts with direct reference to the action of individuals. As to human nature (ONTO-3), it tends to be read through an ontology of the Homo Economicus: the rational choice, utility maximiser social agent of the neo-classical economics, whose roots can be traced to the philosophy of utilitarianism, which lies at the roots of many of the claims of the NPM (Ongaro, 2020, pp. 177–179). Individual agency is important, yet social structures may also prove highly influential, with a thrust of the NPM to design institutions which may leverage on structural conditioning to create 'rules of the game' for individual agency to pursue self-regarding, maximising behaviours.

Finally, and like for OPA, a Newtonian-Galilean conception of time and space (ONTO-2) can align ideationally to the NPM. Neo-positivism or a traditional realist or a critical realist ontology may be deemed as broadly compatible with the NPM (ONTO-1).

An ideational Public Governance Configuration of the New Public Governance and Collaborative Governance

The burgeoning strand of literature of the so-called Collaborative Governance and the set of doctrines ascribed to the New Public Governance—introduced more directly in contrast to the NPM—can be seen as both a post- and an anti-NPM set of administrative doctrines. Key tenets in this approach—although these are also distinct streams of literature and strands in their own right—are the literature on the co-production of public services and, more recently, on the co-creation of solutions to public affairs problems. The emphasis in this strand is on the notion of *public governance* (Peters & Pierre, 2000); indeed, this very set of doctrines contains a range of nuances of meaning which are conveyed through the English-language word of *governance* which may not have an exact correspondent in other languages (see Ongaro & van Thiel, 2018b). Citizens-users of public services take up multiple roles and agency in this set of doctrines: they perform as co-producers of public services or co-creators of innovative solutions to public affairs problems; they wield agency in shaping public decision-making.

A range of constitutional-philosophical doctrines may align with the NPG/CG, albeit with qualifications, and definitely not all (POLPHIL-9). Constitutional Liberalism and Liberal Democracy is broadly aligned with it (indeed, NPG/CG is often seen as a way of revitalising it), but certain strands of Liberal Democracy get especially emphasised, notably deliberative and especially participatory democracy, while others are rather seen as pre-requisite but incomplete on their own (notably, Representative Democracy). Traditional Republicanism with its emphasis on civic participation can be seen as broadly aligned with NPG/CG. Radical Democracy (à la Mary Parker Follett) can be seen as closely related: indeed, Follett's thought may constitute an intellectual source for at least some strands of NPG/CG. Direct Democracy with its emphasis on self-governing and direct participation to public decision-making may also be seen as broadly aligned potentially, yet the literature on NPG/CG hardly makes mention of it (to our knowledge). On the other hand, Libertarian Liberalism, with its emphasis on leaving the individual alone and keeping the state out of her/his life as much as possible, is hardly compatible with NPG/CG. Socialism (Social Democracy) is also aligned with NPG/CG. Much less aligned is Communism, in all its variants, at least to the extent that the state takes on a central role in governing society. Equally incompatible with the core tenets of NPG/CG are the political doctrines of Fascism and Absolutism, with their emphasis on the individual leader or the collective dominant group taking control of all public affairs and administering it in a top-down, authoritarian fashion: the state here manages public services, but hardly entrusts its subjects to act on par with the bureaucracy in the delivery of such services, let alone in their governance and decision-making processes.

While different from—if not outright opposed to—the NPM in terms of contents and substantive orientation, the NPG shares with the NPM a similar thrust in terms of legitimacy of public administration and administrative action not being a given, rather being in urgent need of recovery, by reforming the public sector: legitimacy (POLPHIL-8) becomes problematic and contested in the NPG as it is in the NPM. However, the NPM and the NPG sharply differ in POL-9 as one of the underpinnings of NPM can be found in Libertarian Liberalism and a vision of citizens (in the sociological sense) not being asked to engage in co-producing and even less so in co-creating, rather to exercise their rights as customers. Conversely, NPG and Collaborative Governance, notably in the co-production and especially co-creation focus (Ansell & Gash, 2008; Torfing et al., 2024) are underpinned by a political philosophy of Participatory Democracy and, possibly, by traditional Republicanism as a political philosophy notably where it emphasises civic participation and engagement by citizens.

In terms of public ethos and the ethics (E-7) underpinning the NPG, the demand posed on public administrators and citizens alike is quite significant: a quasi-heroic ethos is predicated of the social actors engaged in making forms of collaborative governance, co-creation and co-production happen—a staunch commitment to devoting oneself to creating or sustaining the common good. The notion of supererogatory action may prove highly meaningful here (Biancu & Ongaro, 2025). Supererogatory actions and attitudes are considered morally positive and yet beyond the call of duty: they are not required nor demandable—they are not object of obligation. According to illustrious philosophers like Thomas Aquinas, they belong to the sphere of the counsels rather than the commandments, and counsels are morally superior to commandments: if the latter concern what is good, the former concern a better good. We would argue that both the public administrator and the citizen alike as conceived of in the NPG/CG are—mostly implicitly—seen as acting beyond the 'mere' call of duty: the ethics of supererogatory applies to them.

As to the language of NPG/CG doctrines (LANG-6), we may expect the language to be in verbs in the gerundial form, emphasising the process through which a solution is being attained (co-created) or a service is being (co-)produced. In terms of underlying epistemology (EPI-5), experiential learning, generating knowledge through acting and experimenting, the lived experience of people engaging into forms of collaborative governance can be as important, if not more, than 'objective', observational knowledge in neo-positivist fashion.

The theory of structuration (Giddens, 1984) and approaches balancing social agency and social conditioning (Archer, 2012) can provide a closely aligned social ontology (ONTO-4). Human nature (ONTO-3), in the perspective of CG/NPG, is deemed to have a natural inclination to the good, benevolent rather than malevolent, generous more than selfish, other-regarding more than self-regarding, virtuous more than vicious.

Human beings are conceived of as free, they are seen as protagonists of their life, but freedom here is not the Libertarian-individualist variant conceived of as the removal of the obstacles that impede the individual to pursue its preferences, rather it is the relational notion of freedom: human beings are seen here eminently as persons, they are free insofar as they relate to each other, they tie their own life and destiny to that of the others, they conceive of themselves as part (and builder) of a community. The 'co-'element, the togetherness that is implied in the process of co-creation as well as of co-production, as well as of collaboration, are premised on an ontology of human nature as centred on a relation conception of person and freedom (Ongaro et al., 2025b). Social structures are influential but individual agency, and notably co-agency of freely interacting individuals, albeit within structural conditioning, takes the lead in this perspective.

Also the conception of space/place and time (ONTO-2) may shift in the perspective of NPG/CG doctrines: time may not anymore be the spatialised time of physics, rather it is the lived time of experience, à la Henry Bergson (1913/1989—on the application of Bergson's thinking to public administration problems, see Ongaro, 2020, pp. 119–123 in particular). Space is the (social) place of human encounters and interactions, where individual liberties meet and connect to each other. Even the very underpinning ontology (ONTO-1) may be different to those associated to the previous sets of doctrines: the very notion of creation in co-creation may be used in the common parlance to mean 'bringing about something', but may also be intended as referring to a different ontological underpinning, an ontology of becoming in which the capacity of human beings to give rise to things that do not exist (at least in the relative sense, as in the absolute sense it is only God who may be attributed the power to create *ex nihilo*, out of nothingness) underpins this set of doctrines.

An ideational Public Governance Configuration of the Neo-Weberian State integrated with Public Value Governance and Management

The 'Neo-Weberian State' (NWS) is a widely debated set of administrative doctrines which has been introduced in the contemporary public administration discourse by Christopher Pollitt and Geert Bouckaert (2004/2017) and qualified, by one of the very authors who coined the notion in the contemporary public administration literature, both as a model and as an ideal type (Bouckaert, 2023).

The Weberian elements in the NWS include a reaffirmation of: (a) the role of the state as the main facilitator of solutions to the new problems posed by globalisation, demographic trends, environmental threat and technological change; (b) the role of representative democracy (central, regional and local) as the legitimating element within the state apparatus; (c) the role of administrative law, suitably modernised, in preserving principles pertaining to the state-citizen relationship (including equality before the law, legal security and the availability of specialised legal scrutiny of state actions); as well as d) the idea of a distinctive status, culture and (to some extent) terms and conditions of the public service (Pollitt & Bouckaert, 2017, p. 121).

Before we review the 'neo' elements of the NWS, we recall here another major set of administrative doctrines, namely Public Value (PV). We follow an approach which proposes to integrate the NWS and PV into one composite framework (Ongaro, 2024), varied according to whether the NWS is considered as a model or an ideal type, and whether PV is conceived of as centred around laying out a structure of practical reasoning to guide public managers in engaging in processes of addition of PV through their agential action undertaken within public service settings (à la Moore, 1995, 2013), or whether it is seen as the outcome of a process of deliberation, by which 'what constitutes value is established dialectically [thereby allowing] for contest, and for diversities of values and identities, within a negotiated understanding of what it means to be part of the wider 'public' sphere, at that time and place' (Benington 2011, p. 43; also Benington, 2015). Within this framework and focusing notably the conception of the NWS as an ideal-type and PV as addition of value through actions by public managers, the 'neo' elements of the NWS integrated with PV can be defined as follows:

a) the shift from an internal orientation towards bureaucratic rules to an external orientation towards meeting citizens' needs actively pursued by entrepreneurial public managers orientated to the creation of Public Value; b) the supplementation (not replacement) of the role of representative democracy by a range of devices for consultation with the direct representation of citizens' views, thereby including a range of tools and heuristics to detect the public values in the political community and gauge and measure the creation of Public Value; c) a modernization of the relevant laws, in the management of resources within government, to encourage a greater orientation on the achievement of results rather than merely the following of correct procedure, thereby enabling or at least facilitating public managers value-creating entrepreneurship; d) a professionalization of the civil service, so that 'bureaucrats' become not simply experts in the law relevant to their sphere of activity, but also they get closer to professional managers, oriented to meeting the needs of their users, and knowledge of the law in the relevant area is only one of a broader range of skills required of a public official, an integral part of which lies in laying out a structure of practical reasoning to enable and guide public managers to the creation of Public Value. In the integration of the NWS as an ideal-type with PV conceived of as addition of value through actions by public managers, the resultant is a further qualified NWS ideal-type, in which PV as a (quasi-) paradigm 'infuses' the NWS and provides additions to it that ultimately produce a more nuanced and articulate ideal-type of the NWS. (Ongaro, 2024, pp. 839–840)

Jointly with the abovementioned Weberian elements, the 'neo' elements summed up in the above quote outline the doctrinal contents of the NWS—PV.

In terms of underlying political philosophy (POLPHIL-9), the NWS-PV is quite selective: it is purposefully meant to be a set of administrative doctrines thought of for the purpose of preserving and strengthening Liberal Democracy, in all its variants. It is, however, at odds with Libertarian Liberalism. It is not thought for, nor compatible with, Radical Democracy and Direct Democracy either. It can fully accommodate Social Democracy, but not Communism in any variant, nor Fascism, nor forms of Absolutism, nor any other non-liberal conception of political regime.

It adopts an intermediate position when it comes to the issue of legitimacy of administrative action (POLPHIL-8). It shares with OPA the same basic assumption whereby the state is legitimate in itself (in this being Hegelian in thrust), and yet it recognises that the public sector has to recover the trust of the people it administers and serves, and the 'neo' elements of the NWS are premised on as well as aimed at attaining such legitimacy, which is therefore considered as problematic, and recovering trust and legitimacy through reforming the public sector is seen as an overarching goal and rationale for the NWS.

In terms of ethical foundations (E-7), there may be an inherent tension between the Weberian component premised on demanding of public administrators to perform their duty 'and nothing more', and the managerial and PV component demanding of public managers to go beyond the 'mere' call of duty—to act in a supererogatory perspective, as is the case of the NPG / CG, to 'go the extra mile' for the ultimate purpose of creating Public Value and restoring the trust of the people in the system.

As to the language of the NWS-PV discourse and rhetoric (LANG-6), this is likely to be a balance of nouns and verbs, of entities and processes, of being (in the Weberian component) and becoming (in the managerial and PV component). Its epistemology (EPI-5) can combine a realist epistemology with more interpretive ones, and in terms of social ontology (ONTO-4) it can accommodate a range of perspectives in terms of balance between social structures influences and individual agency. The model of human being (ONTO-3) is one which combines the sense of duty expected of the traditional bureaucrat with the (supererogatory in thrust) orientation to performing beyond the call of duty, possibly underpinned by a natural inclination to the good and a conception of human beings—or at least those human being who (self-select and) choose to commit to living their professional life in the public service—as other-regarding more than self-regarding. Also the foundational conceptions of time-space/place and being (ONTO-1 and ONTO-2) may be seen as combining—in perhaps not an easy equilibrium—a more 'traditional' realist ontology with a conception of time as the lived time of experience (Bergson, 1913/1989) and space as the social place of human encounters and interactions, where individual creativity may unfold and bring about the creation of public value.

An ideational Public Governance Configuration of the Guardian State

In an attempt to rethink the role of the bureaucracy as defender of Liberal Democracy, Yesilkagit et al. (2024) have wrought out a set of conditions conducive to making the (core) civil service to perform as a guardrail to prevent liberal-democratic regimes to slide into any other form of political regime (so-called democratic backsliding). They call it the 'Guardian State'. In this framework, the bureaucracy is tasked with a higher-order competence to protect the liberal-democratic constitution should this be menaced, thereby elevating public administration to the status of a 'fourth branch of the state', alongside Montesquieu's traditional separation of public powers along the executive, legislative and judiciary divide. The authors then outline the features the civil service must possess to be able to discharge this higher-order function, if circumstances arise, including the ways in which the recruitment, selection and training occurs, in order to socialise civil servants into this core mandate by educating and training civil servants not only to develop skills to deliver public policies, but also to enable them to detect and counter challenges to the liberal-democratic constitution, and they outline a training and educational path for civil servants in which public ethics and political philosophy become core components, in an institutional framework of higher level of bureaucratic autonomy.

It is a bit of a stretch to liken the Guardian state to a full-fledged set of administrative doctrines, when in effect this contribution has at its core one specific preoccupation (albeit a gargantuanly important one), namely delineating the characteristics the civil service must possess to be able to prevent democratic backsliding and preserve liberal democracy (where it is already in place), should this be threatened. We therefore single out for analytical purposes only the political-philosophical under-pinnings (POLPHIL-8 and POLPHIL-9) of this partial and focused set of administrative doctrines, hinging around the one preoccupation of preventing liberal democracies to undergo democratic backsliding, as these are constitutive of this governance configuration. In terms of constitutional-political doctrines (POLPHIL-9), the Guardian State is by definition compatible only with Liberal Democracy, albeit in all its variants, thereby encompassing also Libertarian Liberalism, alongside Social Democracy meant as a set of doctrines emphasising social justice with the framework of Liberal Democracy. The Guardian State is, by definition, antithetical—contrived exactly for the purpose of contrasting—all authoritarian forms of political system, and indeed broadly all non-liberal political regimes. It is also hardly compatible with forms of radical Democracy or Direct Democracy. Legitimacy of the public sector and administrative action is a given for the Guardian state (POLPHIL-8); indeed the 'reform' of the public sector which is argued for by this set of administrative doctrines aims exactly at 'locking in' the liberal-democratic political regime as being legitimate in and by itself.

By way of concluding reflection on this ideational public governance configuration, it may be observed that in a number of important regards, the Neo-Weberian State (previous section) and the Guardian State could be combined, resulting in the NWS with—however—a different role for the bureaucracy in regard to its role, which gets to be redefined to escape subordination to political institutions (*pace* Weber!) insofar as it comes to protecting the state itself: a conception of the bureaucracy as itself a political institution and a 'branch' of the state on par with the others, by having the bureaucracy to embody and protect the liberal-democratic state also from itself. In performing such function of protecting the liberal-democratic states from internal, domestic forces pushing for democratic backsliding (though it may be noticed in many factual instances such domestic forces pushing in the direction of democratic backsliding get supported by the deliberate interference of external non-democratic or outright anti-democratic states and other foreign actors), the bureaucracy is granted constitutionally protected prerogatives.

DISCUSSION AND CONCLUSION

This chapter provides a map to navigate the broader and multi-layered ideational context into which public administration research, discourse and practices are embedded. It does so by pointing out nine ideational dimensions and suggesting conceiving of administrative doctrines as best understood when seen as embedded into the ten-fold ideational public governance configuration which constantly and dynamically shapes the ways in which public administration is thought of in the given 'here and now', at any given moment and place where human beings live their lives in 'administered societies'.

We have illustrated the notion by examining five ideational public governance configurations, taken because of their significance in contemporary debates and which are amply debated, but ultimately in only an illustrative fashion to discuss the application of the notion of ideational public governance configurations, as more administrative doctrines have currency, or will have in the future.

The key message we propose and offer for consideration to the reader in this chapter is that the adoption of a broad philosophical perspective to understand and frame the ideational bases of PADS may be an apt way to both enlarge and better underpin the comparative knowledge of public administration. Administrative doctrines are a form of knowledge which is normative in thrust, whereby knowledge about how things are gets deployed to prompt and compel change towards how things ought to be, a desired end-state about the functioning of public administration and the configuration of the public sector at large. This chapter suggests the use of the notion of ideational public governance configuration to indicate the overall configuration of administrative doctrines (with their inherent normative-prescriptive thrust) together with the ideas—ontological, epistemological, linguistic, ethical-moral and political philosophical—which enable to underpin, conceptualise, interpret and explain administrative doctrines. The notion of ideational public governance configuration is therefore a conceptual tool, informed by the adoption of a philosophical perspective, for unpacking and elucidating the ideational bases of our understanding of public administration as well as addressing normative-prescriptive issues about how the public sector ought to be organised.

REFERENCES

Achten, V., Bouckaert, G., & Schokkaert, E. (Eds.). (2016). *A Truly Golden Handbook: The Scholarly Quest for Utopia*. Leuven University Press.

Al-Amoudi, I., & O'Mahoney, J. (2016). Ontology: Philosophical Discussion and Implications for Organizational Studies. In R. Mir, H. Wilmott, & M. Greenwood (Eds.), *The Routledge Companion to Philosophy in Organization Studies* (pp. 15–32). Routledge.

Alford, R. (2008). 'The Limits to Traditional Public Administration or Rescuing Public Value from Misrepresentation', *Australian Journal of Public Administration, 38*(2), 130–148.

Alford, J., & O'Flynn, J. (2009). Making Sense of Public Value. *International Journal of Public Administration, 32*(3–4), 171–191.

Ansell, C., & Alison, G. (2008). 'Collaborative governance in theory and practice'. *Journal of Public administration Research and Theory, 18*(4), 543–571

Archer, M. S. (2012). *The Reflexive Imperative*. Cambridge University Press.

Barzelay, M. (2001). *The New Public Management. Improving Research and Policy Dialogue*. University of California Press.

Benington, J. (2011). From Private Choice to Public Value? In J. Benington & M. H. Moore (Eds.), *Public Value: Theory and Practice*. Palgrave Macmillan.

Benington, J. (2015). Public Value as a Contested Democratic Practice. In J. M. Bryson, B. C. Crosby, & L. Bloomberg (Eds.), *Creating Public Value in Practice* (pp. 29–48). CRC Press.

Benington, J., & Moore, M. (2011). *Public Value: Theory and Practice*. Palgrave Macmillan.

Bergson, H. (1913/1989). *Essai sur les Données Immediates de la Conscience [Time and Free Will]* (F. L. Pogson, Trans.). George Allen and Co.

Bird, C. (2006). *An Introduction to Political Philosophy*. Cambridge University Press.

Bouckaert, G. (2020a). From Public Administration in Utopia to Utopia in Public Administration. In G. Bouckaert & W. Jann (Eds.), *European Perspectives for Public Administration: The Way Forward* (pp. 71–84). Leuven University Press.

Bouckaert, G. (2020b). Foreword. In E. Ongaro (Ed.), *Philosophy and Public Administration: An Introduction* (pp. vii–ix). Edward Elgar.

Bouckaert, G. (2023). The Neo-Weberian State: From Ideal Type Model to Reality? *Max Weber Studies, 23*(1), 13–59.

Bozeman, B. (2007). *Public Values and Public Interest: Counterbalancing Economic Individualism.* Georgetown University Press.

Bryson, J., Crosby, B., & Bloomberg, L. (Eds.). (2015). *Creating Public Value in Practice: Advancing the Common Good in a Multi-Sector, Shared-Power, No-One-Wholly-In-Charge World.* Taylor and Francis.

Chapman, R. A. (2003). Ethics and Accountability in Public Service. *Teaching Public Administration, 23*(1), 15–26.

Cordelli, C. (2020). *The Privatized State.* Princeton University Press.

De Graaf, G., Huberts, L., & Smulders, R. (2016). Coping with Public Value Conflicts. *Administration and Society, 48*(9), 1101–1127.

Denahrdt, J. V., & Denhardt, R. D. (2015). *The New Public Service—Serving, Not Steering* (4th ed.). Routledge.

Downs, A. (1965). A Theory of Bureaucracy. *The American Economic Review, 55*(1/2), 439–446.

Drechsler, W. (2020). Postscript to the Second Edition: Philosophy in and of Public Administration Today, Global-Western and Non-Western. In E. Ongaro (Ed.), *Philosophy and Public Administration: An Introduction* (pp. 296–302). Edward Elgar.

Dunleavy, P. (1991). *Democracy, Bureaucracy and Public Choice: Economic Explanations in Political Science.* Harvester Wheatsheaf.

Dunleavy, P., & Hood, C. (1994). From Old Public Administration to New Public Management. *Public Money and Management, 14*(3), 9–16.

Dunleavy, P., Margetts, H., Bastow, S., & Tinkler, J. (2006). *Digital Era Governance: IT Corporations, the State, and E-government.* Oxford University Press.

Elder-Vaas, D. (2010). *The Causal Power of Social Structures.* Cambridge University Press.

Frederickson, H. G. (1980). *The New Public Administration.* University of Alabama Press.

Giddens, A. (1984). *The Constitution of Society: Outline of the Theory of Structuration.* University of California Press.

Hartley, J., Alford, J., Knies, E., & Scott, D. (2017). Towards an Empirical Research Agenda for Public Value Theory. *Public Management Review, 19*(5), 670–685.

Heath, J. (2020). *The Machinery of Government: Public Administration and the Liberal State*. Oxford University Press.

Hood, C. (1991). A Public Management for All Seasons? *Public Administration*, *69*(1), 3–19.

Howell, K. E. (2012). *An Introduction to the Philosophy of Methodology*. Sage.

Meynhardt, T. (2009). Public Value Inside: What Is Public Value Creation. *International Journal of Public Administration*, *32*, 192–219.

Moore, M. (1995). *Creating Public Value. Strategic Management in Government*. Harvard University Press.

Moore, M. (2013). *Recognizing Public Value*. Harvard University Press.

Niskanen, W. A. (1973). *Bureaucracy: Servant or Master*. Institute of Economic Affairs.

Niskanen, W. A. (1994). *Bureaucracy and Public Economics*. Edward Elgar Publishing.

Ongaro, E. (2019). The Teaching of Philosophy for Public Administration Programmes. *Teaching Public Administration*, *37*(2), 135–146. https://doi.org/10.1177/0144739419837310

Ongaro, E. (2020). *Philosophy and Public Administration: An Introduction*. Edward Elgar. Available open access [also translated into Chinese, Italian, Portuguese and Spanish] (first edition 2017).

Ongaro, E. (2021). 'Non-Western Philosophies and Public Administration', Guest Editorial. *Asia Pacific Journal of Public Administration*, *43*(1), 6–10. https://doi.org/10.1080/23276665.2020.1844027

Ongaro, E. (2022a). Philosophy for and of Public Administration and Management. In *Elgar Encyclopaedia of Public Management*. Elgar Publishing.

Ongaro, E. (2022b). The Fourfold Nature of Public Administration as Science, Art, Profession, and Humanism: Implications for Teaching. In K. A. Bottom, J. Diamond, P. T. Dunning, & I. C. Elliott (Eds.), *Handbook of Teaching Public Administration* (pp. 26–34). Edward Elgar Publishing. https://doi.org/10.4337/9781800375697.00014

Ongaro, E. (2024). Integrating the Neo Weberian state and Public Value. *International Review of Administrative Sciences*, *90*(4), 830–844. https://doi.org/10.1177/00208523241228830

Ongaro, E. (2025). The Arts and Public Administration: How the Consideration of the Nature of Art Can Provide Novel Ways to Understand Public Administration. In E. Ongaro, G. Orsina, & L. Castellani (Eds.), *The Humanities and Public Administration: An Introduction* (pp. 207–216). Edward Elgar.

Ongaro, E. (2026). *Interdisciplinary Approaches and Context Analysis in Public Administration*. Bingley.

Ongaro, E., Orsina, G., & Castellani, L. (Eds.). (2025a). *The Humanities and Public Administration: An Introduction*. Edward Elgar.

Ongaro, E., Rubalcaba, L., & Solano, E. (2025b). The Ideational Bases of Public Value Co-creation and the Philosophy of Personalism: Why a Relational Conception of Person Matters for Solving Public Problems. *Public Policy and Administration, 40*(3), 429–451.

Ongaro, E., & van Thiel, S. (Eds.). (2018a). *The Palgrave Handbook of Public Administration and Management in Europe.* Palgrave Macmillan.

Ongaro, E., & van Thiel, S. (2018b). Languages and Public Administration in Europe. In E. Ongaro & S. van Thiel (Eds.), *The Palgrave Handbook of Public Administration and Management in Europe* (pp. 61–98). Palgrave.

Osborne, S. P. (2006). The New Public Governance?. *Public Management Review, 8*(3), 377–387. https://doi.org/10.1080/14719030600853022

Pierre, J., & Guy Peters, B. (2000). *Governance, Politics and the State.* Palgrave Macmillan.

Pollitt, C. (Ed.). (2013). *Context in Public Policy and Management: The Missing Link?* Edward Elgar.

Pollitt, C., & Bouckaert, G. (2017). *Public Management Reform. A Comparative Analysis: Into the Age of Austerity* (4th ed.). Oxford University Press.

Rhodes, R.A.W., & Wanna, J. (2007). 'The Limits to Public Value or Rescuing Responsible Government from the Platonic Guardians'. *Australian Journal of Public Administration, 66*(4), 406–421.

Rhodes. R.A.W and Wanna, J. (2008) 'Bringing The Politics Back In: Public Value in Westminster Parliamentary Government'. *Public Administration, 87*(2), 161-83.

Roberts, A. (2011). *The Logic of Discipline: Global Capitalism and the Architecture of Governments.* Oxford University Press.

Torfing, J., Ferlie, E., Jukić, T., & Ongaro, E. (Eds.). (2024). *Strategic Management of the Transition to Public Sector Co-Creation.* Bristol University Press.

Wilson, E. O. (1998). *Consilience: The Unity of Knowledge.* Alfred A. Knopf.

Yesilkagit, K., Michael Bauer, B., Peters, G., & Pierre, J. (2024). The Guardian State: Strengthening the Public Service Against Democratic Backsliding. *Public Administration Review, 84*(3), 414–425. https://doi.org/10.1111/puar.13808

Zacka, B. (2022). Political Theory Rediscovers Public Administration. *Annual Review of Political Science, 25*(1), 21–42.

CHAPTER 5

Philosophy of Public Administration

Abstract This chapter undertakes the task of defining and delineating the contours of a philosophy of public administration (PA) which may be fit for the problems and challenges of PA in the twenty-first century. Philosophy of PA is identified as a branch of philosophy which is derivative (i.e. it is grounded on foundational areas of philosophy, such as ontology or epistemology or political philosophy) and whose main task is elaborating the research questions in PA that are philosophical in nature, thereby outlining what is distinctively philosophical in PA problems and questions. It is further argued that a philosophy of PA may draw upon one very important strand of philosophical thinking in the Aristotelian-Thomistic philosophical tradition which has been fleshed out through very distinctive contributions provided by such philosophers like Francis Bacon, Thomas Hobbes and Giambattista Vico, who coined the expression 'verum factum est', that is, what is true in the social world is such because it has been made, we know it because we humans are its maker, we have made it and thereby we are the cause of it. This encapsulates the idea of a maker's conception of philosophy, which is central to the philosophy of information theorised by Luciano Floridi and which can provide a valuable blueprint for working out a philosophy of PA.

Keywords Philosophy · Public administration · Philosophy of public administration · Administrative science · Administrative theory · Philosophical system

© The Author(s) 2026   121
E. Ongaro, *Connecting Philosophy and Public Administration*,
Foundations of Government and Public Administration 1,
https://doi.org/10.1007/978-3-032-01769-7_5

Introduction, Rationale and Definition

This chapter addresses the direction of inquiry in the relationship between philosophy and PA which is possibly the most intellectually challenging, as well as fascinating, namely, defining and delineating the contours of what *a philosophy of public administration for the twenty-first century* may look like (to notice we use 'PA' to encompass the fields of public administration, public management, public governance and government, referring to both the scholarly study and the practice of it—see Chapter 1 for further discussion of definitions and terminology).

In a very schematic way, we may consider there are two main senses in which it can be spoken of a philosophy *of* PA:

(i) Philosophy of PA as a 'section' of a broader philosophical system.
(ii) Philosophy of PA as a dedicated philosophical elaboration.

Regarding the former sense in which it is possible to speak of a philosophy of PA, possibly the most notable example in (western) philosophy is the Philosopher Georg Wilhelm Hegel's *Theory of Right*, which contains a section dedicated to PA (Paras 287–297) and more amply incorporates the study of bureaucracy and administration organically within the author's broader philosophical system. We qualify this example (exemplar) as 'notable' for two reasons: due to the prominent standing of the German philosopher, as well as due to it being quite a rarity in the history of philosophy that a major philosophy book includes a section specifically dedicated to PA.

It is, however, in relation to the latter sense in which it is possible to speak of a philosophy of PA that this chapter unfolds: the contours of philosophy of PA as a dedicated philosophical elaboration (and not as a 'section' of a broader philosophical system) are outlined in this chapter, which is therefore centred on the profiling of what a philosophy of PA may look like as a dedicated intellectual enterprise for the needs of the contemporary epoch: a philosophy of PA for the twenty-first century.

The argument wrought out here is patterned on Floridi (2011 and 2019), whose framework to work out what he calls the philosophy of information—another 'branch' of philosophy very significant for addressing contemporary problems—is taken as a blueprint. There are two complementary reasons why Floridi's philosophy of information and his approach to philosophical questioning is taken as a blueprint here.

The first reason is the sheer effectiveness and clarity of his elaboration of a branch of philosophy as such; the second and complementary reason is that the philosophy of information may be extremely pertinent for contemporary PA, for a philosophy of PA for the twenty-first century.

The latter point—that the philosophy of information may be a pertinent pattern for working out a philosophy of PA for the twenty-first century—can be argued on multiple grounds. Because, like philosophy of information, philosophy of PA is oriented to address socially and culturally contextual problems (PA as problem-driven). It is pertinent also because, here again akin to philosophy of information as conceptual design (see Floridi, 2019), PA is action-oriented—PA can be seen also as a profession and a praxis (Raadschelders, 2008), and hence a notion of philosophy as conceptual design may be an appropriate way of conceiving of philosophy of PA. Furthermore, because PA is part of the built/artificial environment, it is a human-made reality: hence the maker's knowledge, the kind of knowledge that derives from being the maker, the 'creator' of something (a strand of philosophical thinking which has its roots in Aristotle and Thomas Aquinas and has been developed by philosophers such as Francis Bacon and Gianbattista Vico), as distinct from the kind of knowledge that derives from observing something (beholder's knowledge), is a central way of knowing in and for PA, like it is in information, of which humans are co-producers (this resonates with the conception of PA as also 'art' as discussed in Chapter 1, see Bouckaert, 2025; de Graaf and van Asperen, 2025; Drechsler, 2025; Ongaro, 2025). Moreover, because PA is inherently concerned with ethical-moral issues, like philosophy of information is (Floridi, 2014). And last but not least, because the 'information revolution' is likely to continue to be a direct shaper of PA—the study, the profession, the art, the practice—in the twenty-first century (and likely beyond).

While our concern is with contemporary problems and contemporary applications of philosophical thinking, we would (dare to) argue that discussion of the following key conceptual components is part and parcel of any philosophy of PA (past, present and future). A philosophy of PA is grounded in performing the following conceptual functions:

(i) appropriately categorising philosophy of PA as a branch within (the much broader field of) philosophy, notably noticing that Philosophy of PA is *philosophia seconda*, i.e. it is derivative, it is not a foundational area of philosophy (*philosophia prima*): it is grounded on the main areas of philosophy, it relies on the key 'findings' (so to speak) of philosophical thinking and then applies it in a derivative way;

(ii) elaborating on philosophy of PA as... philosophy proper, that is, characterized by the fact that it appropriates a specific *ti esti* (in ancient Greek) / *quid est* (in Latin), that is, a specific 'what is', a specific domain of reality; notably it does so by addressing in a philosophical manner the two defining issue of PA: what is 'public(ness)', and what is 'administration'; as philosophy proper, philosophy of PA aspires to be an attractor of investigation, that is, it is a mediator of inquiry: it is a centre piece of intellectual investigation in order to be foundational to other and related intellectual efforts that rely on philosophical underpinnings; and it attracts, or at least facilitates and enriches, investigation in both the field of philosophy and the field of PA (in simple words: it is an intellectual effort that bears fruits—it is 'fruitful');

(iii) elaborating the research questions (hereafter: RQs) in PA that are philosophical in nature, rather than addressable through social sciences methods, thereby outlining what is distinctively philosophical in PA problems and questions;

(iv) working out a philosophical approach to enable addressing such RQs, to address those RQs in PA that are philosophical in nature.

The performance of the above conceptual functions is the *raison d'être* of a philosophy of PA, the hallmark of it being a philosophy proper. In fact, by performing the above functions a philosophy of PA can (i) situate itself within the broader field of philosophy; (ii) identify and define the domain of reality it addresses; (iii) identify the research questions in PA that are philosophical in nature, as distinct from those which are answerable via social (or other) science methods and approaches; and (iv) address, by the means and approaches proper of philosophy (Kenny, 2010, chapter 1), the research questions in PA that are philosophical in nature.

We can suggest a tentative *definition* of Philosophy of PA (again, patterned on Floridi's blueprint of the philosophy of information) as follows: '*a philosophical field concerned with the critical investigation of the*

conceptual nature and key concepts and basic principles of public admin-
istration, including its science,[1] methods and problems – as well as the
elaboration and application of theoretical concepts and practical problems
of PA to philosophical problems'.

The remainder of this chapter addresses the key building blocks of this
conceptualisation of philosophy of PA.

PHILOSOPHY OF PA AS *PHILOSOPHIA SECONDA*

We notice that philosophy of PA is *philosophia seconda* (Latin for: 'second-
order philosophy'): it is derivative, it is not a foundational area of
philosophy like ontology, or epistemology, or moral or political philosophy—it is not a *philosophia prima* (foundational in nature). A philosophy
of PA can only draw its concepts and the premises of its philosophising
from the main areas of philosophy, on which it is grounded; its way of
building arguments relies on philosophy *tout court.*

More specifically, philosophy of PA 'mediates' between areas of philosophy as *philosophia prima* (the basic branches of philosophy, such as:
ontology; epistemology; moral philosophy and ethics; philosophy of
mind; or the very philosophy of information we here use as a blueprint)
and the field of PA. The notion of *philosophia seconda* means that philosophy of PA relies upon the concepts and notions of the key branches of
philosophia prima (first order philosophy), it is anchored to the theorising
and the very conceptual and noetic resources furnished by philosophia
prima ('noetic' is a term originating in ancient Greek and amply used
in philosophy, which can loosely be translated as 'intellectual', from the
Greek *noein,* to think, and *nous,* mind, referring to the action of thinking
and the mental act of intellection, and more broadly it can be used to
mean the gaining of knowledge, wisdom, understanding).

To appreciate the significance of it, we may consider that, as a whole,
philosophy of PA mediates between the field of philosophy and the field
of PA. As a further qualification of this claim, it may be appreciated that
philosophy of PA can mediate between specific branches of philosophy

---

[1] We should here specify that by 'science' in philosophy it is meant knowledge obtained
through rigorous methods, knowledge that is grounded and can be claimed to be acquired
with certainty. The term science does not refer here to a specific discipline (like any of the
social sciences) which is defined having its object of investigation and problems formulated
and unproblematically stated and its concepts and methods uncontroversially standardized.

and certain thematic areas in the field of PA which are more closely interlinked; so, for example, philosophy of PA can enable a better connection between: the field of philosophy of Information *and* the field of e-government and digital governance (considered as a field of PA); or between the field of philosophy of mind *and* the field of Behavioural Public Administration; or between moral philosophy and ethics *and* the thematic area studying street-level bureaucracy discretion and state-citizen interactions (Zacka, 2017); and so forth.

PHILOSOPHY OF PA AS PHILOSOPHY PROPER

We have suggested above that, in order to be a philosophy proper, philosophy of PA has to appropriate a specific domain of reality, a defined 'what is'. To this purpose, a philosophy of PA has to engage with issues of ontology (or, at least, with questions which are ontic in nature), i.e. it has to concern itself with addressing issues about the nature of the things it speaks about: what is a 'public entity'; what is (public) 'administration'; what is 'publicness' in public administration; and so forth.

One way of doing it is by addressing in a philosophical manner the two defining issue of PA: what is 'public', or better what is 'publicness', and what is 'administration[2]', and all the derivative of the root word: what is 'administering', what is 'administrator'—and relatedly if one considers that we use the expression 'PA' to refer not only to public administration, but also to notions such as 'public management' or 'public governance': what is 'management', what is 'managing'; and what is 'governance' and 'governing', and so forth (there is clearly more than just a flavour of analytical philosophy and the philosophy of language in this way of approaching the ontological question). The political philosophical and philosophy of law notions of public sphere, public space, public value (in the singular) and public values (plural), public purpose, legitimacy (and relatedly the notions of common good, social contract and social justice),

---

[2] The root word of the English language term 'administration derives from the Latin word *ad*, which means 'to', and *ministrare*, which can be translated as 'to provide service', 'to be at the service of', yet more specifically the Latin root word for minister or ministering means (being) 'minor', (being) 'less than' (those who are served), hence *administration* as the act of being at the service of by operating from a position of inferiority towards what is being served, that is, the public.

legality, rights and duties (of the citizen and of the human being), ethicality and morality all pertain to defining issues of PA from a philosophical standpoint. It is the task of the (yet-to-be-worked out in full) philosophy of PA to be able to investigate philosophically the defining issues of PA.

The ontological grounding provided by a philosophy of PA must display (and the 'success' of a philosophy of PA to live up to what can be expected of it can be gauged against) the following properties:

- being 'sufficiently' portable, i.e. general enough to be applicable across the field's sub-areas—for example, the ontological grounding of key issues around the nature of publicness of public administrations should be applicable to underpin the investigation of topics ranging from the sub-area of performance management in the public sector to that of the organisation of the public sector, and so forth;
- being scalable, i.e. the 'solutions' it generates continue to work and 'hold' also when the complexity or magnitude of the problem increases; and
- being interoperable across the field of PA, i.e. the capacity of an ontology to allow interactions between different theories (Floridi, 2011, Sect. 15.4 in particular—notice these concepts have been worked out borrowing from the vocabulary of computer science), even 'distant' ones.

A similar way of framing these properties is by asserting that a philosophy of PA must possess the extent, scope and width of a regional ontology. In fact, in terms of ontology, philosophy of PA can be seen as a regional ontology located within the realm of social ontology. Social ontology is a branch of ontology, a regional ontology whose focus is on the nature and foundations of *social entities* ('the study of what sort of things exist in the social world and how they relate to each other', Elder-Vass, 2010, p. 4). Philosophy of PA is an ontology which is concerned with the nature of PA entities and their relations (the word 'structures'—PA entities and their structures—may also be used here). As a specific regional ontology, it posits minimal ontological commitment in terms of general ontology (e.g. it does not require to answer the 'foundational' ontological questions of, e.g. whether reality is monistic or dualistic or else; whether reality is material or ideal or informational or all of these; whether reality is ultimately about objects and their properties as manifest to a knowing subject and/ or it is about their relations/structures; and similar questions).

In terms of epistemology (in fact, a philosophy of PA has to concern itself with and engage in issue of epistemology: What can be known, and how?), a philosophy of PA demands the knowability of relations and/or the empirical manifestations of PA entities, but it can be quite agnostic and limitedly demanding from an epistemic viewpoint re the foundations of knowledge (whether in a realist or transcendental or constructivist or constructionist perspective, and so forth). Yet, crucially, a philosophy of PA must be productive: it must be fruitful, that is (as Floridi suggests it be the case for the philosophy of information he so decisively contributed to establish), it must be capable of addressing pressing, relevant, contemporary problems—it therefore must have a capacity of generating knowledge and understanding that would not otherwise be available without it (In simpler words: a philosophy of PA has to be able to make the difference in the knowledge and understanding of PA).

Another related feature for philosophy of PA to be a philosophy proper is for philosophy of PA to aspire to be an attractor of investigation; that is, it is a mediator of inquiry: it is a centrepiece of intellectual investigation, in order to be able to provide foundations for other intellectual efforts to build upon (or adopting a humbler and less ambitious characterisation, it must at least be sufficiently influential to withstand centrifugal forces, that is, to be relevant for intellectual inquires in the field not to bypass it, or not entirely at least). Philosophy of PA must be able to attract, or at least facilitate and enrich, investigation in both the field of philosophy and the field of PA—it needs to be 'fruitful'.

The characterisation provided so far of what a philosophy of PA should look like might seem quite formalistic-abstract: being about the formal properties and contours of a philosophy of PA. Yet philosophy has been made over the millennia by the work of Philosophers—real people who have made this inquiry into the most fundamental questions that human beings may ask. The reader might then rightly ask at this point to 'name the names': Which Philosophers may be an inspiration for working out the philosophy of PA?

This is of course no easy question, but we would like here to suggest one path. We argue that, in terms of 'broad strands' of philosophy, any future philosophy of PA may draw upon, and owe much to, one very important strand of philosophical thinking, which may be qualified as 'a maker's conception of philosophy'. This strand lies in the Aristotelian-Thomistic philosophical tradition and it has been fleshed out through very distinctive contributions provided by such philosophers like Francis Bacon and Thomas Hobbes and, crucially, Giambattista Vico, who coined the expression *verum factum est*, that is, what is true in the social world is such because it has been made, we know it because we are its maker, we have made it and thereby we are the cause of it. This encapsulates the idea of a maker's conception of philosophy. It is an approach recently revitalised by Luciano Floridi (whose work is yet again employed as blueprint), who has developed a constructionist (not constructivist) notion of philosophy as conceptual design (Floridi, 2019), a philosophical perspective which may provide a pathway for grounding a philosophy of PA for the twenty-first century, the century of the information age.

Towards a System of Research Questions in Public Administration That Are Philosophical in Nature

Delineating a philosophy of PA entails shifting the focus of the analysis from research questions (RQs) which are 'social scientific' in kind, i.e. they can be addressed (answered) through social science contents and methods, and towards questions which are philosophical in kind. The first key task for a philosophy of PA is therefore to clarify what are philosophical questions.

In order to be philosophical, questions—and therefore the philosophical questions of a philosophy of PA: the 'PA philosophy questions'—should possess the following features (Floridi, 2019, chapter 1):

- being *open* to informed, rational and honest disagreement;
- being *ultimate, but not absolute*;
- being *closed under further questioning*;
- being *constrained by empirical and logical-mathematical reasoning but requiring noetic resources to be answered*.

These features are here discussed. First, philosophical questions are *open* to informed, rational and honest disagreement. This definition can be appreciated by contrasting it with social scientific research (in PA as elsewhere) which—in principle at least—aims for the attainment of answers that are 'closed', in the sense that they are answered exhaustively and thence there is no need to further investigate such questions (however infrequent this may happen to be in the practice in PA research, this is the ambition of social sciences, like any sciences: to 'close' the question by exhaustively answering it). As Floridi phrases this point: 'What I am suggesting is that empirical and logico-mathematical questions are such that, once we have the necessary and sufficient resources to formulate a correct answer, any further disagreement on that formulated answer may speak volumes about the parties involved but says nothing about the answer itself' (Floridi, 2019, p. 8). By contrast, being philosophical, PA philosophical questions remain open, which does not mean they cannot and indeed should not be answered, but it is their inherent nature (so to speak) that any answer remains open to informed, rational and honest disagreement (see more broadly Floridi, 2019, chapter 1, for a dissection of the features open questions possess, and a critical discussion to a range of possible objections).

An example here will suffice: the author of this book was graciously invited to join a research programme lasted over many years investigating the features displayed by 'public agencies', defined as semi-autonomous organisations carrying out public tasks. The overarching goal of the research programme was to study public agencies in European countries as well as at the European Union level level, and investigate empirically and conceptually their relative autonomy from their parent organisation and the way in which they are steered and controlled and held accountable, as well as the way in which they form their own (constrained) strategy and the ways in which they participate to the public policy process (this research produced countless publications—for an overview and a thoughtful compendium of some of the main findings, see Verhoest et al., 2012). The reader may well imagine the innumerable hours discussing what is 'public' in and of a public agency, the question of what makes an organisation 'public'. However, in hindsight we (or at least I) may have been too shy and reluctant in fully engaging with the underlying issue of the notion of publicness: if there is one area in which this otherwise so comprehensive research programme might have gone further is in revisiting the political-philosophical debate on publicness and privateness—what is public and what is private and where one sphere ends and the other begins (for a composite review of this notion by PA academics for application to PA problems and issues, see Whetsell et al., 2025).

Philosophy would have helped this research programme. The issue of 'publicness' (and its complementary notion of 'privateness') is an intellectual issue with a very long history of being debated in philosophy, both in the West and in the East. By way of hinting to the complexity and articulation of the philosophical debate, Plato's famous—and provocative—approach consists in suppressing the private interest (and the private dimension *tout court*) almost entirely, as suggested in his work *The Republic* in which he puts in the mouth of the character Socrates (generally representing Plato's view in his dialogues) the controversial proposal—the 'noble lie'—of telling everyone in the city (the political community in ancient Greece) that they were born not from their parents but by the land and earth of their city, who is therefore mother of all, de facto abolishing the institution of the family altogether (hence de facto suppressing almost entirely the private dimension of its citizens) and raising the children and looking after the elders in a totally communitarian way; as a consequence, the rulers and the guardians of the city will treat the elders (who may be their parents) or the young (who may be their children) as if they were their parents or children (and indeed such they might be), so that that rulers cannot favour their own kins (the 'private interest') and rather they will be restrained in how they treat everyone else by the fear of disfavouring their very own ancestors or progeny. Yet western philosophical thinking, or at least the main strands of liberalism as they have developed in the West, have not followed this route, rather have settled on dealing with the issue of defining the private (sphere) and the public (sphere) by means of drawing a clear, neat distinction if not outright separation between the public and the private, in the direction of demarcating and separating the two as much as possible, also as an intellectual strategy to deal with the conflicts that may arise between the two—and when conflicts arise, a more prevailing thrust in western liberal thinking has been to protect the private as much as possible from the public 'intruding' into it. Other western political philosophies, like Marxism, have proceeded the other way around while yet others philosophical streams, quite distinct and in other regards different between them, like traditional Republicanism or Christian Personalism, have focused more on a harmonious combination or even (moderate) fusion between the two, whereby the cultivation of both private and public virtues (ultimately virtues *tout court*) is indispensable and mutually reinforcing to protect both the public and the private sphere, and ultimately for the betterment of society. All of these philosophies, however, tend to assume a demarcation between the public and the private.

In the East, the issue of what is public (public sphere, public interest) and what is private has been dealt with differently. Notable is the Confucian view whereby the private and the public are seen as part of a continuum, rather than being neatly distinguished, with hierarchisation of one's duties as the intellectual strategy to deal with conflicts that arise between the private and the public sphere: the 'Confucian continuum and harmony model', as Bai (2020, p. 138) calls it, is an intellectual framework within which solutions on how to harmonise the public and the private are found to be contextual rather than generally applicable (thereby also entailing a risk of contextualism and ad hoc-only and patchy solutions). It is however important to notice the pluralism of strands of thinking in Chinese philosophical debate, whereby other political philosophers, notably Han Fei Zi, sharply and eloquently argued (against Confucius and Mencius) that the public and the private are fundamentally in contrast, thereby entailing that the private interest will inevitably prevail, unless laws can be formulated and enforced to constrain humans' behaviours (a thinking much in line with, in western political philosophy, Thomas Hobbes's thinking about the state of nature in which human beings are a threat to each other—*homo homini lupus* ('the human being is like a wolf to fellow human beings')—and the 'Leviathan' state becomes a necessary evil to stem human wicked and malevolent inclinations). Yet other intellectual traditions may be evoked to shed light (or perhaps enhance the confusion given the wide range of viewpoints) on the issue of the nature of publicness, like the Islamic intellectual elaboration, which emphasises the primacy of the public dimension to a larger extent than can be found in other religious-philosophical and intellectual traditions, whether Christianity, Confucianism or Buddhism or others.[3]

The moral of the story of our brief excursus into the philosophical treatment of the issue of the nature of publicness is that in order to root 'standard social science research' in PA—like the investigation of public agencies—it is necessary to also address foundational questions about the nature of public agencies, notably what is meant by their 'publicness'

---

[3] Incidentally, we may also notice that PA scholarly work properly referencing and elaborating upon the work of philosophy scholarship may help build true interdisciplinarity, by showing how PA scholars recognise the contribution of other disciplines, notably in philosophy, and can therefore help make this a two-way street, as philosophy-informed PA studies may be structured in such way that they may also inform philosophical investigation.

and what it implies for their operations. This example illustrates how PA philosophical questions are part and parcel of PA scholarly inquiry. It also indicates the sense in which they possess the feature of being open to informed, rational and honest disagreement (we have seen the different conceptions of the public-private relationship that have been elaborated over the millennia in philosophical thinking).

The second feature of PA philosophical questions is that they are *ultimate, but not absolute*. They are ultimate in the sense that they go to the roots of a(ny) PA problem (otherwise they wouldn't be philosophical), but they are not absolute because they are pitched at a specific level of abstraction (on the methods of the level of abstraction, see Floridi, 2011), i.e. they do not apply irrespectively of the level of granularity or detail at which they are pitched. An important qualification here is that, being philosophy of PA a *philosophia seconda* (as we have seen above, and unlike philosophy of information which aims to be *philosophia prima*), philosophical questions in PA are ultimate for (in relation to) PA problems, they are not (or at least they may not necessarily be) ultimate from the perspective of a *philosophia prima* (they are roots questions for PA, but they may be closer to the branches and leaves rather than the roots when seen from the perspective of a philosophia prima: in the example we have seen of public agencies, it is addressed the question of what is the publicness of public agencies: this is an ultimate question for PA, yet not necessarily ultimate nor, especially, absolute, for the broader philosophical debate of the nature of publicness and privateness and their relationship as such, when considered across all the domains of human life and not just in relation to public agencies).

Third, PA philosophical questions are *closed under further questioning*, in the sense specified by Floridi (2019) that they are at the roots of concatenations of questions: answering ultimate questions leads to answering a range of concatenated lower level questions, but lower level questions trigger further questions, while questions closed under further questioning, if and when answered, do not trigger further questions at the same level.

Fourth, PA philosophical questions are *constrained by empirical and logical-mathematical reasoning but requiring noetic resources to be answered*, that is, requiring distinctive purely intellectual-philosophical— as opposed to empirical—resources. In other words, they cannot be answered either by empirical investigation or by logical-mathematical analysis only: they are (also) a matter of informed exchange of rational arguments (Floridi, 2011, chapter 2 and 15). As in the example of what makes a public agency 'public', this question cannot be answered only on empirical ground (although the answer may well be informed also by empirical findings), nor is it frameable in a purely logical-mathematical way—it requires noetic resources and can only be addressed via informed exchanges of rational arguments.

It is beyond the reach of this chapter to work out a system of inter-related PA philosophical questions. Elaborating in full a system of inter-related philosophical questions would be tantamount to fully fleshing out a (or perhaps even *the*) philosophy of PA for the twenty-first century—a task for another book (as such task can only be fulfilled through a wide-scope, systematic, book-length dedicated work, delving into foundational philosophical problems and informed by philosophical process). In line with the purpose and thrust of this book, namely delineating directions of inquiry for connecting the fields of philosophy and the field of PA, we here only recall what the defining features of PA philosophical questions are: being open, ultimate, closed under further questioning at least at the level of a *philosophia seconda*, and requiring noetic resources—as we have seen above.

We can also here briefly point to some aspects of the form such questions can take: being philosophical, they will investigate issues of essence or nature of things, ontological and foundational 'what is' type of questions about PA entities, relations and structures. Alongside being about the 'formal causes' (to borrow from Aristotle's terminology and system of the four causes, see chapter 1), they will probe the rationale of PA-entities, they will take the form of 'why' questions and be about the 'final causes' of PA entities. They will be questions linking PA to thematic areas of *philosophia prima*, like ontology, epistemology, philosophical anthropology, ethics and axiology, political philosophy, as well as newer branches of *philosophia prima* like philosophy of information. Other, distinct yet related, PA Philosophical questions will be about epistemology of PA: What can we know in PA? And how can we know? Intriguingly, since the very process of generating novel knowledge creates new 'facts', as acutely argued by Bouckaert (2020b, p. viii), we may also evoke (albeit in a metaphorical sense rather than in an ontological sense strictly meant) the perspective of causative epistemology (à la Meister Eckhart, see Griffionen 2023, Sect. 6.2 in particular) to make sense of how 'PA entities' get to be known and thence become part and parcel of PA and its philosophy (Bouckaert, 2020b).

Yet other PA philosophical questions will be about individual freedom and social agency in relation to bureaucratic discretion and decision-making (see the discussion of Hegel's and Weber's conceptions of freedom and bureaucracy outlined by Tijsterman & Overeem, 2008, and the significance of a relational conception of freedom for an understanding of the foundations of processes of co-creation of public value discussed by Ongaro et al., 2025b—we have reported on both works in Chapter 2). Yet other and interconnected PA philosophical questions will revolve around normative issues along the perspectives of the branches of philosophy of axiology, ethics and morality—questions of 'what should I do?' and relatedly: 'What can I hope?' as it comes to individual's obligations and expectations in relation to the public sphere, thus, within the realm of the philosophy of PA: What should civil servants do? What are duties and obligations of public officials? What is 'good' public governance? And what can we hope for (rather than despair)? Addressing such questions will involve political-philosophical questions of 'how to live well together?' and notably the PA-related question of how the public sector 'ought to' be reformed so as to contribute to bettering our living together in politico-administrative communities as human beings and so forth.

Applications of a Philosophy of PA and Concluding Remarks

We have here sketched the contours of what a philosophy of PA may look like. Once a philosophy of PA will have been fully developed—a big task ahead—it will complement and supplement, by providing its roots and foundational elements, the social scientific study of PA (Van Thiel, 2014) as well as the practice of it, the practice of PA as a profession, as an art, and as a form of practical humanism (see Chapter 1 and Ongaro, 2020). This task of delineating the profile of the philosophy of PA will be open-ended, both conceptually, that is, open to informed, rational and honest disagreement which will lead to it being dialectically redefined, and temporally, that is, open to be continuously adapted to the evolving circumstances, to make the philosophy of PA a living body of understanding and knowledge fit for the contemporary challenges. Ultimately, the very philosophy of PA that will be elaborated will have to be continuously adjusted and adapted via philosophical querying.

The elaboration of a philosophy *of* PA may enable revisiting the thought of some of the more 'philosophically-minded' scholars of PA, like

Dwight Waldo, whose work can also be read as an investigation into the conceptual nature and key concepts and basic principles of public administration (i.e.: publicness, in all its declensions; administration, in all its declensions). The working out of a philosophy of PA for the twenty-first century may also enable to revisit in a more systematic way the thought of the intellectual founding fathers of PA—a long list including Confucius, Hegel, Nizām al-Mulk, Waldo, Weber, Wolff, *inter alia*—and rediscover the philosophical elements there—for example, the 'Socratic' element contained into Waldo's scholarly work (Overeem, 2025).

Once fully developed, a philosophy of PA will enable to address such PA philosophical questions in relation to the PA problems and themes which are relevant and salient for the twenty-first century, in order to support the development of PA (referring here both to the field of study of PA and the practice of it). A philosophy of PA for the twenty-first century will thus enable to shed light on the assumptions and premises of PA (enlightening function of philosophy applied to PA); to critically revisit such assumptions and premises (critical function); to provide constructs and approaches to fill, at least partly, the gaps in PA assumptions, notions and theories (gap filling function); to facilitate the integration of the multiple disciplinary perspectives that are employed to address public administration problems and themes, also by shedding light on the philosophical residue inherent in each discipline as applied to PA (integrative function); and to provide rationales for prescriptive arguments about how the public sector ought to be organised or reorganised (the normative function of philosophy applied to PA).

Finally, we can also ask if and how the elaboration of a philosophy of PA can provide an entry point also for the field of PA to inform, or at least stimulate, the revisiting of issues in the (academic) field of philosophy, that is, alongside the direction from philosophy to PA—central to this book—also the direction from PA to philosophy, we argue, could be a fruitful direction of inquiry. A philosophy of PA should 'feed into' philosophy *tout court*, or at least certain areas of philosophy like political philosophy or public ethics. We have kept this element into the very definition of philosophy of PA where we complete our definition of philosophy of PA by indicating at the end of its definition: '*as well as the elaboration and application of theoretical concepts and practical problems of PA to philosophical problems*' (we recall the definition of philosophy of PA, introduced above: 'a philosophical field concerned with the critical investigation of the conceptual nature and key concepts and basic principles of public administration, including its science, methods and problems – as well as the elaboration and application of theoretical concepts and practical problems of PA to philosophical problems'). We deem this qualification to be part and parcel of the very definition of philosophy of PA, to be constitutive of it. Indeed, as the saying goes that 'when parents beget children, then also the parents change', such metaphor may well apply here: when the field of philosophy begets (the specific subfield of) the philosophy of PA, then also philosophy, as its parent, changes, at least a bit.

The intellectual journey of this book has led us to cross four bridges connecting philosophy and PA. The first bridge we have crossed is the direction of inquiry of philosophy *for* PA, whereby philosophies and philosophical streams get mobilised and employed, individually or in a combined way, for complementing and supplementing knowledge and understanding of PA. The second bridge has led us to walk the opposite direction, proceeding backwards by tracing the philosophical roots of the extant scientific works in the field of public administration, to unveil their underlying philosophical premises and underpinnings. Walking through the third bridge has enabled to address the issue of the alignment between administrative doctrines ('prescriptions' for reforming the public sector) and their ideational bases, which are inherently philosophical. Finally, in the most classic 'last but not least', the fourth bridge—which is yet to be fully built, but the bridgehead has hopefully been positioned in this chapter—has brought us towards the delineation of the contours of a philosophy *of* PA for the twenty-first century.

References

Bai, T. (2020). *Against Political Equality: The Confucian Case*. Princeton University Press.

Bouckaert, G. (2020a). From Public Administration in Utopia to Utopia in Public Administration. In G. Bouckaert & W. Jann (Eds.), *European Perspectives for Public Administration: The Way Forward* (pp. 71–84). Leuven University Press.

Bouckaert, G. (2020b). Foreword. In E. Ongaro (Ed.), *Philosophy and Public Administration: An Introduction* (pp. vii–ix). Edward Elgar.

Bouckaert, G. (2025). Mind the Gap: A Strategy to connect Humanities (Arts) with Social Sciences (Public Administration). In E. Ongaro, G. Orsina, & L. Castellani (Eds.), *The Humanities and Public Administration: An Introduction* (pp. 253–274). Edward Elgar.

de Graaf, G., & van Asperen, H. (2025). The Arts and Public Administration: How Artworks Can Be a Source of Knowledge, Inspiration, Motivation, and Understanding in Public Administration. In E. Ongaro, G. Orsina, & L. Castellani (Eds.), *The Humanities and Public Administration: An Introduction* (pp. 217–235). Edward Elgar.

Drechsler, W. (2025). Ambrogio Lorenzetti's Siena Frescoes and Public Administration Today. In E. Ongaro, G. Orsina, & L. Castellani (Eds.), *The Humanities and Public Administration: An Introduction* (pp. 236–252). Edward Elgar.

Elder-Vaas, D. (2010). *The Causal Power of Social Structures*. Cambridge University Press.

Floridi, L. (2011). *The Philosophy of Information*. Oxford University Press.

Floridi, L. (2014). *The Ethics of Information*. Oxford University Press.

Floridi, L. (2019). *The Logic of Information: A Theory of Philosophy as Conceptual Design*. Oxford University Press.

Griffionen, A. (2023). Meister Eckhart. In *Stanford Encyclopaedia of Philosophy*. https://plato.stanford.edu/entries/meister-eckhart/. Accessed 27 February 2025.

Kenny, A. (2010). *A New History of Western Philosophy*. Oxford University Press.

Ongaro, E. (2020). *Philosophy and Public Administration: An Introduction*. Edward Elgar. Available open access [also translated into Chinese, Italian, Portuguese and Spanish] (first edition 2017).

Ongaro, E. (2025). The Arts and Public Administration: How the Consideration of the Nature of Art Can Provide Novel Ways to Understand Public Administration. In E. Ongaro, G. Orsina, & L. Castellani (Eds.), *The Humanities and Public Administration: An Introduction* (pp. 207–216). Edward Elgar.

Ongaro, E., Orsina, G., & Castellani, L. (Eds.). (2025a). *The Humanities and Public Administration: An Introduction*. Edward Elgar.

Ongaro, E., Rubalcaba, L., & Solano, E. (2025b). The Ideational Bases of Public Value Co-creation and the Philosophy of Personalism: Why a Relational Conception of Person Matters for Solving Public Problems. *Public Policy and Administration, 40*(3), 429–451.

Overeem, P. (2025). Socratic Public Administration: The Relevance of Dwight Waldo Today. In E. Ongaro, G. Orsina, & L. Castellani (Eds.), *The Humanities and Public Administration: An Introduction* (pp. 23–35). Edward Elgar.

Raadschelders, J. (2008). Understanding Government: Four Intellectual Traditions in the Study of Public Administration. *Public Administration, 86*(4), 925–949.

Tijsterman, S. P., & Overeem, P. (2008). Escaping the Iron Cage: Hegel and Weber on Bureaucracy and Freedom. *Administrative Theory & Praxis, 30*(1), 71–91.

Van Thiel, S. (2014). *Research Methods in Public Administration and Public Management: An Introduction*. London: Routledge.

Verhoest, K., Van Thiel, S., Laegreid, P., & Bouckaert, G. (Eds.). (2012). *Government Agencies. Practices and Lessons from 30 Countries*. Palgrave Macmillan.

Whetsell, T., Prebble, M., Raadschelders, J., Pederson, K. Z., Ansell, C., Han, H., Shields, P. M., Hartley, J., Benington, J., & Moore, M. (2025). 'Roundtable: Perspectives on the *Public. Perspectives on Public Management and Governance*. https://doi.org/10.1093/ppmgov/gvaf006

Zacka, B. (2017). *When the State Meets the Street: Public Service and Moral Agency*. Harvard University Press.

REFERENCES

Achten, V., Bouckaert, G., & Schokkaert, E. (Eds.). (2016). *A Truly Golden Handbook: The Scholarly Quest for Utopia*. Leuven University Press.

Al-Amoudi, I., & O'Mahoney, J. (2016). Ontology: Philosophical Discussion and Implications for Organizational Studies. In R. Mir, H. Wilmott, & M. Greenwood (Eds.), *The Routledge Companion to Philosophy in Organization Studies* (pp. 15–32). Routledge.

Alford, J., & O'Flynn, J. (2009). Making Sense of Public Value. *International Journal of Public Administration, 32*(3–4), 171–191.

Ansell, C. (2025). Public Philosophy and the Administrative State. In E. Ongaro, G. Orsina, & L. Castellani (Eds.), *The Humanities and Public Administration: An Introduction* (pp. 36–50). Edward Elgar.

Archer, M. S. (2012). *The Reflexive Imperative*. Cambridge University Press.

Atkinson, R. F. (1978). *Knowledge and Explanation in History: Introduction to the Philosophy of History*. Cornell University Press.

Bai, T. (2020). *Against Political Equality: The Confucian Case*. Princeton University Press.

Baldoli, R., & Radaelli, C. M. (2022). Unity in Fragility: Nonviolence and COVID-19. *Italian Political Science Review/Rivista Italiana di Scienza della Politica, 52*(3), 378–390. https://doi.org/10.1017/ipo.2021.38

Barzelay, M. (2001). *The New Public Management. Improving Research and Policy Dialogue*. University of California Press.

Bauer, M. (2018). Public Administration and Political Science. In E. Ongaro & S. van Thiel (Eds.), *The Palgrave Handbook of Public Administration and Management in Europe* (pp. 1049–1065). Palgrave Macmillan.

© The Author(s) 2026

E. Ongaro, *Connecting Philosophy and Public Administration*,
Foundations of Government and Public Administration 1,
https://doi.org/10.1007/978-3-032-01769-7

Beaton, E. E., Raadschelders, J. C. N., Wilson, G. D., Khurana, S., & Leach, N. R. (2024). The Yoke of Objectivity in Public Administration (and Beyond). *Perspectives in Public Management and Governance, 7*(3), 89–100.

Benington, J. (2011). From Private Choice to Public Value? In J. Benington & M. H. Moore (Eds.), *Public Value: Theory and Practice*. Palgrave Macmillan.

Benington, J. (2015). Public Value as a Contested Democratic Practice. In J. M. Bryson, B. C. Crosby, & L. Bloomberg (Eds.), *Creating Public Value in Practice* (pp. 29–48). CRC Press.

Benington, J., & Moore, M. (2011). *Public Value: Theory and Practice*. Palgrave Macmillan.

Bergson, H. (1913/1989). *Essai sur les Données Immediates de la Conscience [Time and Free Will]* (F. L. Pogson, Trans.). George Allen and Co.

Biancu, S., & Ongaro, E. (2025). Benevolence, Public Ethics and Public Services: Revisiting Public Value, Public Service Motivation, and Models of Public Administration Through the Ethics of Supererogation. In E. Ongaro, G. Orsina, & L. Castellani (Eds.), *The Humanities and Public Administration: An Introduction* (pp. 68–78). Edward Elgar.

Bird, C. (2006). *An Introduction to Political Philosophy*. Cambridge University Press.

Bouckaert, G. (2020a). From Public Administration in Utopia to Utopia in Public Administration. In G. Bouckaert & W. Jann (Eds.), *European Perspectives for Public Administration: The Way Forward* (pp. 71–84). Leuven University Press.

Bouckaert, G. (2020b). Foreword. In E. Ongaro (Ed.), *Philosophy and Public Administration: An Introduction* (pp. vii–ix). Edward Elgar.

Bouckaert, G. (2023). The Neo-Weberian State: From Ideal Type Model to Reality? *Max Weber Studies, 23*(1), 13–59.

Bouckaert, G. (2025). Mind the Gap: A Strategy to connect Humanities (Arts) with Social Sciences (Public Administration). In E. Ongaro, G. Orsina, & L. Castellani (Eds.), *The Humanities and Public Administration: An Introduction* (pp. 253–274). Edward Elgar.

Bozeman, B. (2007). *Public Values and Public Interest: Counterbalancing Economic Individualism*. Georgetown University Press.

Brown, B. E. S., & Stillman, R. J., II. (1986). *A Search for Public Administration: The Ideas and Career of Dwight Waldo*. A&M University Press.

Bryson, B. C., & Bloomberg, L. (Eds.). (2015). *Creating Public Value in Practice: Advancing the Common Good in a Multi-Sector, Shared-Power, No-One-Wholly-In-Charge World*. Taylor and Francis.

Bryson, J., Crosby, B., & Bloomberg, L. (2014). Public Value Governance: Moving Beyond Traditional Public Administration and the New Public Management. *Public Administration Review, 74*(4), 445–456.

Capitini, A. (1998). *Scritti filosofici e religiosi*. Fondazione Centro Studi Aldo Capitini.

Capitini, A. (2000). A Philosopher of Nonviolence. *Diogenes, 48*, 104–119.

Carroll, J. D., & Frederickson, H. G. (2001). Dwight Waldo, 1913–2000. *Public Administration Review, 61*(1), 2–8.

Cassese, S. (1993). *Il sistema amministrativo italiano*. il Mulino.

Chapman, R. A. (2003). Ethics and Accountability in Public Service. *Teaching Public Administration, 23*(1), 15–26.

Chapman, R., & Lowndes, V. (2014). Searching for Authenticity? Understanding Representation in Network Governance: The Case of Faith Engagement. *Public Administration, 92*(2), 274–290.

Cordelli, C. (2020). *The Privatized State*. Princeton University Press.

De Graaf, G., Huberts, L., & Smulders, R. (2016). Coping with Public Value Conflicts. *Administration and Society, 48*(9), 1101–1127.

de Graaf, G., & van Asperen, H. (2025). The Arts and Public Administration: How Artworks Can Be a Source of Knowledge, Inspiration, Motivation, and Understanding in Public Administration. In E. Ongaro, G. Orsina, & L. Castellani (Eds.), *The Humanities and Public Administration: An Introduction* (pp. 217–235). Edward Elgar.

Denahrdt, J. V., & Denhardt, R. D. (2015). *The New Public Service—Serving, Not Steering* (4th ed.). Routledge.

Dewandre, N., & Ongaro, E. (2022). L'Administration Européenne au défi de la philosophie (et inversement) [The European Administration and the Challenge of Confronting Itself with Philosophy—And Vice Versa], *Revue Française d'Administration Publique*, n.180. [also translated into English and in press as chapter 2 as 'European administration challenged by philosophy (and vice versa)'. In D. Georgakakis (Ed.) (2024), *The Changing Topography of EU Administration: Organisations, Actors and Policy Processes*. Palgrave.

Di Nuoscio, E. (2003). *Methodological Individualism, Scientific Explanation, and Hermeneutics*. In N. Bulle & F. Di Iorio (Eds.), *The Palgrave Handbook of Methodological Individualism*. Palgrave.

Di Nuoscio, E. (2018). *The Logic of Explanation in the Social Sciences*. Bardwell Press.

Di Nuoscio, E. (2025). Epistemology and Public Administration: A Trial-and-Error Approach. In E. Ongaro, C. Barbati, F. Di Mascio, F. Longo, & A. Natalini (Eds.), *Public Administration in Italy: The Science and the Profession*. Palgrave.

Drechsler, W. (2020). Postscript to the Second Edition: Philosophy in and of Public Administration Today, Global-Western and Non-Western. In E. Ongaro (Ed.), *Philosophy and Public Administration: An Introduction* (pp. 296–302). Edward Elgar.

Drechsler, W. (2025). Ambrogio Lorenzetti's Siena Frescoes and Public Administration Today. In E. Ongaro, G. Orsina, & L. Castellani (Eds.), *The Humanities and Public Administration: An Introduction* (pp. 236–252). Edward Elgar.

Downs, A. (1965). A Theory of Bureaucracy. *The American Economic Review, 55*(1/2), 439–446.

Dunleavy, P. (1991). *Democracy, Bureaucracy and Public Choice: Economic Explanations in Political Science.* Harvester Wheatsheaf.

Dunleavy, P., & Hood, C. (1994). From Old Public Administration to New Public Management. *Public Money and Management, 14*(3), 9–16.

Dunleavy, P., Margetts, H., Bastow, S., & Tinkler, J. (2006). *Digital Era Governance: IT Corporations, the State, and E-government.* Oxford University Press.

Dwivedi, O. P. (1990). Administrative Theology: Dharma of Public Officials. *Indian Journal of Public Administration, 36*(3), 406–419.

Elder-Vaas, D. (2010). *The Causal Power of Social Structures.* Cambridge University Press.

Ferlie, E., Lynn, L. E., & Pollitt, C. (Eds.). (2005). *The Oxford Handbook of Public Management.* Oxford University Press.

Floridi, L. (2011). *The Philosophy of Information.* Oxford University Press.

Floridi, L. (2014). *The Ethics of Information.* Oxford University Press.

Floridi, L. (2019). *The Logic of Information: A Theory of Philosophy as Conceptual Design.* Oxford University Press.

Fourcade, M., Ollion, E., & Algan, Y. (2015). The Superiority of Economists. *Journal of Economic Perspectives, 29*(1), 89–114.

Frederickson, H. G. (1980). *The New Public Administration.* University of Alabama Press.

Giddens, A. (1984). *The Constitution of Society: Outline of the Theory of Structuration.* University of California Press.

Griffionen, A. (2023). Meister Eckhart. In *Stanford Encyclopaedia of Philosophy.* https://plato.stanford.edu/entries/meister-eckhart/. Accessed 27 February 2025.

Hartley, J., Alford, J., Knies, E., & Scott, D. (2017). Towards an Empirical Research Agenda for Public Value Theory. *Public Management Review, 19*(5), 670–685.

Heath, J. (2020). *The Machinery of Government: Public Administration and the Liberal State.* Oxford University Press.

Hegel, G. W. F. (1991). *Elements of the Philosophy of Right* (H. B. Nisbet, Trans.). Cambridge University Press. (Original work published 1821)

Hood, C. (1991). A Public Management for All Seasons? *Public Administration, 69*(1), 3–19.

Howell, K. E. (2012). *An Introduction to the Philosophy of Methodology.* Sage.

Huberts, L. (2014). *The Integrity of Governance: What It Is, What We Know, What Is Done, and Where to Go*. Palgrave Macmillan.

Jorgensen, T. B., & Rutgers, M. R. (2015). Public Values: Core or Confusion? Introduction to the Centrality and Puzzlement of Public Values Research. *The American Review of Public Administration, 45*(1), 3–12.

Kasulis, T. (2025). Japanese Philosophy. In E. N. Zalta & U. Nodelman (Eds.), *The Stanford Encyclopedia of Philosophy* (Spring 2025 Edition). https://plato.stanford.edu/archives/spr2025/entries/japanese-philosophy/

Kenny, A. (2010). *A New History of Western Philosophy*. Oxford University Press.

Lynch, T. D., & Cruise, P. L. (Eds.). (2006). *Handbook of Organization Theory and Management: The Philosophical Approach* (First edition, 1998). CRC Press.

Lynn, L. E., Jr. (2006). *Public Management: Old and New*. Routledge.

Meynhardt, T. (2009). Public Value Inside: What Is Public Value Creation. *International Journal of Public Administration, 32*, 192–219.

Moore, M. (1995). *Creating Public Value. Strategic Management in Government*. Harvard University Press.

Moore, M. (2013). *Recognizing Public Value*. Harvard University Press.

Nagatomo, S. (2025). Japanese Zen Buddhist Philosophy. In E. N. Zalta & U. Nodelman (Eds.), *The Stanford Encyclopedia of Philosophy* (Spring 2025 Edition). https://plato.stanford.edu/archives/fall2024/entries/japanese-zen/

Ni, Y., & Liu, N. (2025). Bridging the Theory-Practice Divide in Public Administration; A Virtuous Pragmatic Approach of Wang Yangming and William James. *Public Policy and Administration, 40*(3), 452–476.

Niskanen, W. A. (1973). *Bureaucracy: Servant or Master*. Institute of Economic Affairs.

Niskanen, W. A. (1994). *Bureaucracy and Public Economics*. Edward Elgar Publishing.

Ongaro, E. (2009). *Public Management Reform and Modernization: Trajectories of Administrative Change in Italy, France, Greece, Portugal and Spain*. Edward Elgar.

Ongaro, E. (2013). Explaining Contextual Influences on the Dynamics of Public Management Reforms: Reflections on Some Ways Forward. In C. Pollitt (Ed.), *Context in Public Policy and Management: The Missing Link?* (pp. 192–207). Edward Elgar.

Ongaro, E. (2019). The Teaching of Philosophy for Public Administration Programmes. *Teaching Public Administration, 37*(2), 135–146. https://doi.org/10.1177/0144739419837310

Ongaro, E. (2020). *Philosophy and Public Administration: An Introduction*. Edward Elgar. Available open access [also translated into Chinese, Italian, Portuguese and Spanish] (first edition 2017).

Ongaro, E. (2021). Non-Western Philosophies and Public Administration, Guest Editorial. *Asia Pacific Journal of Public Administration, 43*(1), 6–10. https://doi.org/10.1080/23276665.2020.1844027

Ongaro, E. (2022a). Philosophy for and of Public Administration and Management. In *Elgar Encyclopaedia of Public Management*. Elgar Publishing.

Ongaro, E. (2022b). The Fourfold Nature of Public Administration as Science, Art, Profession, and Humanism: Implications for Teaching. In K. A. Bottom, J. Diamond, P. T. Dunning, & I. C. Elliott (Eds.), *Handbook of Teaching Public Administration* (pp. 26–34). Edward Elgar Publishing. https://doi.org/10.4337/9781800375697.00014

Ongaro, E. (2024). Integrating the Neo Weberian state and Public Value. *International Review of Administrative Sciences, 90*(4), 830–844. https://doi.org/10.1177/00208523241228830

Ongaro, E. (2025). The Arts and Public Administration: How the Consideration of the Nature of Art Can Provide Novel Ways to Understand Public Administration. In E. Ongaro, G. Orsina, & L. Castellani (Eds.), *The Humanities and Public Administration: An Introduction* (pp. 207–216). Edward Elgar.

Ongaro, E. (2026). *Interdisciplinary Approaches and Context Analysis in Public Administration*. Bingley, UK: Emerald.

Ongaro, E., & Ho, T. K. A. (2025). Eastern and Western Philosophies: Rethinking the Foundations of Public Administration. *Public Policy and Administration, 40*(3), 403–411. https://doi.org/10.1177/09520767251330456

Ongaro, E., Orsina, G., & Castellani, L. (Eds.). (2025a). *The Humanities and Public Administration: An Introduction*. Edward Elgar.

Ongaro, E., Rubalcaba, L., & Solano, E. (2025b). The Ideational Bases of Public Value Co-creation and the Philosophy of Personalism: Why a Relational Conception of Person Matters for Solving Public Problems. *Public Policy and Administration, 40*(3), 429–451.

Ongaro, E., & Tantardini, M. (2023a). *Religion and Public Administration: An Introduction*. Edward Elgar. https://www.e-elgar.com/shop/gbp/religion-and-public-administration-9781800888029.html

Ongaro, E., & Tantardini, M. (2023b). Advancing Knowledge in Public Administration: Why Religion Matters, Guest Editorial. *Asia Pacific Journal of Public Administration*. https://doi.org/10.1080/23276665.2022.2155858

Ongaro, E., & Tantardini, M. (2024a). Contours of a Research Programme for the Study of the Relationship of Religion and Public Administration. *Public Policy and Administration, 39*(4), 521–530. https://doi.org/10.1177/09520767241272897

Ongaro, E., & Tantardini, M. (2024b). Religion, Spirituality, Faith and Public Administration: A Literature Review and Outlook. *Public Policy and Administration, 39*(4), 531–555. https://doi.org/10.1177/09520767221146866

Ongaro, E., & Tantardini, M. (2024c). Bringing Religion into Public Value Theory and Practice: Rationale and Perspectives. *Administration and Society*. https://doi.org/10.1177/00953997241264474

Ongaro, E., & van Thiel, S. (Eds.). (2018a). *The Palgrave Handbook of Public Administration and Management in Europe*. Palgrave Macmillan.

Ongaro, E., & van Thiel, S. (2018b). Languages and Public Administration in Europe. In E. Ongaro & S. van Thiel (Eds.), *The Palgrave Handbook of Public Administration and Management in Europe* (pp. 61–98). Palgrave.

Ongaro, E., & Yang, Y. (2025). Integrating Philosophical Perspectives into the Study of Public Administration: The Contribution of Critical Realism to Understanding Public Value. *Public Policy and Administration, 40*(3), 477–496. https://journals.sagepub.com/doi/10.1177/09520767241246654

Ostrom, V. (2008). *The Intellectual Crisis in American Public Administration* (3rd ed.). University of Alabama Press.

Overeem, P. (2025). Socratic Public Administration: The Relevance of Dwight Waldo Today. In E. Ongaro, G. Orsina, & L. Castellani (Eds.), *The Humanities and Public Administration: An Introduction* (pp. 23–35). Edward Elgar.

Parboteeah, K. P., Paik, Y., & Cullen, J. B. (2009). Religious Groups and Work Values: A Focus on Buddhism, Christianity, Hinduism, and Islam. *International Journal of Cross Cultural Management, 9*(1), 51–67.

Perry, J. L., & Christensen, R. K. (2015). *Handbook of Public Administration*. Jossey-Bass.

Pierre, J., & Guy Peters, B. (2000). *Governance, Politics and the State*. Palgrave Macmillan.

Pollitt, C. (Ed.). (2013). *Context in Public Policy and Management: The Missing Link?* Edward Elgar.

Pollitt, C. (2016). *Advanced Introduction to Public Management and Administration*. Edward Elgar Publishing.

Pollitt, C., & Bouckaert, G. (2017). *Public Management Reform. A Comparative Analysis: Into the Age of Austerity* (4th ed.). Oxford University Press.

Popper, K. R. (1935/1992). *The Logic of Scientific Discovery*. Routledge.

Popper, K. R. (1994). Science: Problems, Aims, Responsibilities. In Id., *The Myth of the Framework: in Defence of Science and Rationality*. Routledge.

Raadschelders, J. (2005). Government and Public Administration: The Challenge of Connecting Knowledge. *Administrative Theory & Praxis, 27*(3), 602–627.

Raadschelders, J. (2008). Understanding Government: Four Intellectual Traditions in the Study of Public Administration. *Public Administration, 86*(4), 925–949.

Raadschelders, J. (2011). *Public Administration: The Interdisciplinary Study of Government*. Oxford University Press.

Riccucci, N. (2010). *Public Administration: Traditions of Inquiry and Philosophies of Knowledge*. Georgetown University Press.

Roberts, A. (2011). *The Logic of Discipline: Global Capitalism and the Architecture of Governments*. Oxford University Press.

Rosenbloom, D. H., Cravchuk, R. S., & R. M. Clerkin (2022). *Public Administration: Understanding Management, Politics and Law in the Public Sector* (9th ed.). Rutledge.

Rosser, C. (2018). Weber's Bequest for European Public Administration. In E. Ongaro & S. van Thiel (Eds.), *The Palgrave Handbook of Public Administration and Management in Europe* (pp. 1011–1029). Palgrave Macmillan.

Rots, A. P. (2016). Reclaiming Public Space: Shinto and Politics in Japan Today. *Proceedings of the International Conference of the Royal Academy for Overseas Sciences—Belgian Institute of Higher Chinese Studies*, 23–45.

Rutgers, M. R. (1998). Paradigm Lost: Crisis as Identity of the Study of Public Administration. *International Review of Administrative Sciences, 64*(4), 553–564.

Ryan, A. (2012). *On Politics. A History of Political Thought from Herodotus to the Present*. Penguin Books.

Sager, F., & Rosser, C. (2009). Weber, Wilson, and Hegel: Theories of Modern Bureaucracy. *Public Administration Review, 69*(6), 1136–1147.

Selznick, P. (1957/1984). *Leadership in Administration: A Sociological Interpretation*. University of California Press.

Sharp, G. (1973). *The Politics of Nonviolent Action. Part One: Power and Struggle*. Porter Sargent Publishers.

Shaw, C. K. Y. (1992). Hegel's Theory of Modern Bureaucracy. *American Political Science Review, 86*, 381–389.

Simon, H. (1946). The Proverbs of Administration. *Public Administration Review, 6*(1, Winter), 53–67.

Tang, L., Li, Z., Liu, H., & Jing, Y. (2025). Appraising the Philosophical Influences on Modern Public Administration Research. *Public Policy and Administration, 40*(3), 513–531. https://doi.org/10.1177/0952076724126 6774

Tantardini, M., & Ongaro, E. (2025). The Contribution of the Religious Studies and Theology Literatures to Public Administration: A Review and Outlook. In E. Ongaro, G. Orsina, & L. Castellani (Eds.), *The Humanities and Public Administration: An Introduction* (pp. 152–175). Edward Elgar.

Tijsterman, S. P., & Overeem, P. (2008). Escaping the Iron Cage: Hegel and Weber on Bureaucracy and Freedom. *Administrative Theory & Praxis, 30*(1), 71–91.

Tong, Z. (2025). Deliberative Mini-publics as a Confucian Institution. *Public Policy and Administration, 40*(3), 412–428.

Tooze, A. (2018). *Crashed: How a Decade of Financial Crises Changed the World.* Penguin.

Torfing, J., Ferlie, E., Jukić, T., & Ongaro, E. (2021). A Theoretical Framework for Studying the Co-creation of Innovative Solutions and Public Value. *Policy and Politics, 49*(2), 189–209.

Torfing, J., Ferlie, E., Jukić, T., & Ongaro, E. (Eds.). (2024). *Strategic Management of the Transition to Public Sector Co-Creation.* Bristol University Press.

Van Thiel, S. (2014). *Research Methods in Public Administration and Public Management: An Introduction.* London: Routledge.

Verhoest, K., Van Thiel, S., Laegreid, P., & Bouckaert, G. (Eds.). (2012). *Government Agencies. Practices and Lessons from 30 Countries.* Palgrave Macmillan.

Wagner, C. S., & Raadschelders, J. (2025). From Disciplinary Depth to Inter-disciplinary Breadth: The Case of Public Administration. *American Review of Public Administration, 55*(4), 299–317.

Waldo, D. (1948/1984). *The Administrative State: A Study of the Political Theory of American Public Administration* (2nd ed.; first published in 1948). Holmes & Meier and Ronald Press.

Waldo, D. (1977). *Democracy, Bureaucracy and Hypocrisy.* Institute of Governmental Studies, University of California.

Waldo, D. (1980). *The Enterprise of Public Administration: A Summary View* (5th ed.). Chandler & Scharp.

Waldo, D. (1990). A Theory of Public Administration Means in Our Time a Theory of Politics Also. In N. B. Lynn & A. Wildavsky (Eds.), *Public Administration: The State of the Discipline* (pp. 73–83). Chatham House.

Weber, M. (1903–1906/2012). *Roscher and Knies and the Logical Problems of Historical Economics* (1903–1906). In H. Henrik Bruun & S. Whimster (Eds.), *Max Weber. Collected Methodological Writings.* Routledge.

Werlin, H. H. (2001). Bureaucracy and Democracy: An Essay in Memory of Dwight Waldo. *Public Administration Quarterly, 25*(3), 290–315.

Whetsell, T. (2025). Philosophical Pragmatism and the Study of Public Administration. In E. Ongaro, G. Orsina, & L. Castellani (Eds.), *The Humanities and Public Administration: An Introduction* (pp. 50–57). Edward Elgar.

Whetsell, T., Prebble, M., Raadschelders, J., Pederson, K. Z., Ansell, C., Han, H., Shields, P. M., Hartley, J., Benington, J., & Moore, M. (2025). 'Roundtable: Perspectives on the *Public. Perspectives on Public Management and Governance.* https://doi.org/10.1093/ppmgov/gvaf006

Wilson, E. O. (1998). *Consilience: The Unity of Knowledge.* Alfred A. Knopf.

Yesilkagit, K., Michael Bauer, B., Peters, G., & Pierre, J. (2024). The Guardian State: Strengthening the Public Service Against Democratic Backsliding.

Public Administration Review, 84(3), 414–425. https://doi.org/10.1111/puar.13808

Yung, B. (2014). In What Way Is Confucianism Linked to Public Service Motivation? Philosophical and Classical Insights. *International Journal of Public Administration, 37*(5), 281–287.

Zacka, B. (2017). *When the State Meets the Street: Public Service and Moral Agency.* Harvard University Press.

Zacka, B. (2022). Political Theory Rediscovers Public Administration. *Annual Review of Political Science, 25*(1), 21–42.

Zhang, X., & He, Y. (2020). What Makes Public Space Public? The Chaos of Public Space Definitions and a New Epistemological Approach. *Administration and Society, 52*(5), 749–770.

Index

© The Author(s) 2026
E. Ongaro, *Connecting Philosophy and Public Administration*,
Foundations of Government and Public Administration 1,
https://doi.org/10.1007/978-3-032-01769-7

MIX

Papier | Fördert
gute Waldnutzung

FSC® C083411

Zeitfracht Medien GmbH
Ferdinand-Jühlke-Straße 7
99095 Erfurt, Deutschland
produktsicherheit@kolibri360.de